A Time to Question Everything

A Time to Question Everything

Embracing Good News and Bad Days

By
BO M. WHITE

WIPF & STOCK · Eugene, Oregon

A TIME TO QUESTION EVERYTHING
Embracing Good News and Bad Days

Copyright © 2018 Bo M. White. All rights reserved. Except for brief quotations in critical publications or reviews, no part of this book may be reproduced in any manner without prior written permission from the publisher. Write: Permissions, Wipf and Stock Publishers, 199 W. 8th Ave., Suite 3, Eugene, OR 97401.

Wipf & Stock
An Imprint of Wipf and Stock Publishers
199 W. 8th Ave., Suite 3
Eugene, OR 97401

www.wipfandstock.com

PAPERBACK ISBN: 978-1-5326-5116-8
HARDCOVER ISBN: 978-1-5326-5117-5
EBOOK ISBN: 978-1-5326-5118-2

Manufactured in the U.S.A.   06/12/18

Scripture quotations are from the ESV® Bible (The Holy Bible, English Standard Version®), copyright © 2001 by Crossway, a publishing ministry of Good News Publishers. Used by permission. All rights reserved.

Scripture quotations marked (NIV) are taken from the Holy Bible, New International Version®, NIV®. Copyright © 1973, 1978, 1984, 2011 by Biblica, Inc.™ Used by permission of Zondervan. All rights reserved worldwide. www.zondervan.com. The "NIV" and "New International Version" are trademarks registered in the United States Patent and Trademark Office by Biblica, Inc.™

Contents

Acknowledgments | vii

Introduction | ix

    1 What Do You Want and Desire? | 1

    2 Am I the Problem? | 12

    3 Do You Want to Live or Die? | 21

    4 Should We Fit In or Find Out? | 29

    5 Who Did You Notice Today? | 36

    6 Why Am I Afraid to Sleep? | 47

    7 How Can We Voice Frustration? | 58

    8 Who Will Rescue Me? | 71

    9 Is God Satisfied? | 86

    10 Are Your Plans Working? | 94

    11 Faith Isn't Normal, is It? | 101

    12 Who Do You Trust? | 116

    13 Is Grace Strong Enough for this World? | 121

    14 Is this Worth the Trip? | 128

Bibliography | 137

Acknowledgments

OVER TWENTY YEARS AGO, David Calhoun taught a class on devotional literature and as the class progressed through the semester, I started to find not only what I believed to be real, but I found a way to express it in ways that finally made sense to me. Within the same time frame, Jerram Barrs taught a small cohort of us how to talk about matters of faith with other people. He reminded us that loving people mattered more than showing off what we think we know. I owe Dr. Calhoun and Jerram Barrs a great deal for both their expertise and their example. I still hope to be more like those men someday.

Stan Jantz and the team at Conversant Life allowed me to explore some of the ideas of this book on a blog platform and I am indebted to Mark Kaech for helping set that up. Leadership at All Souls Presbyterian in Champaign, Illinois, and Redeemer Presbyterian in Waco, Texas, have been willing to have conversations about suffering, grace, and how all this crashes into our daily life. These conversations continue to mean a great deal to me and have sharpened some of the ideas. Thanks to All Souls and Redeemer for the chance to give a couple talks related to this stuff. The tribe at Mockingbird Ministries has been fresh air along the way and the generosity of the Mockingbird team has been inspiring to see as well as experience.

Laura Kilgore made this book presentable and her expert insights made this book better. I am truly grateful for Laura, her work, and her editorial eye. I would not have made it to the finish

Acknowledgments

line without her. Matt Wimer and the editorial team at Wipf and Stock made this all come together and I'm humbled by the chance to give this life.

Tami, Alister, and Eliana all feel the weight of my ups and downs and the depths of whether I'm growing in grace or not. I think they know I'm a mess more than anyone else. I'm glad we're making the journey together.

Any mistakes or errors in this book are all mine.

Introduction

AM I HEADING IN the right direction?

I am much quicker at stopping the car and asking for directions these days. I used to stubbornly want to figure things out on my own no matter how long I wandered the countryside. I also used to think that the stranger giving directions may be unreliable and he or she would just say something so I'd leave. Deep down, I just didn't want to ask a dumb question.

I can already hear some of you say that there is no such thing as a dumb question, and there's some truth to that. Where we agree wholeheartedly is that questions are never a dumb idea. It's how we learn. It's how experiments are run and how major events happen.

Before lovers are engaged to be married, someone pops the question. Sherlock Holmes became the world's greatest detective because he asked a lot of questions. Classic philosophers taught their students through using a series of questions. Doctors ask you a lot of questions when they see you to make a proper diagnosis. I think you get the point.

I don't think I would be a Christian if kind people didn't take the time to answer my questions. Even so, my own struggles as a human being in a broken world cause me to wonder if this whole Christianity thing is worth it. Is the gospel true? How can I believe good things and feel so badly at times?

Through reading, conversation, and counseling over the years, I have come to the conclusion that the distinguishing mark of the Christian faith is the gospel of God's grace and that so far,

Introduction

grace has been the most excellent answer to life's hardest questions. If I can extend grace and express love, then it's been a good day.

What's my problem, then? Why am I such a mess?

Honestly, how I feel doesn't always match what I think or believe or aspire to be. I feel exhausted a lot. I feel like I emotionally go up and down like the stock market. Anger, sadness, arousal, and cynicism abound, and there seems to be no end to the changing tides of my ability to curiously think myself into a frenzy.

For some people, eating junk food helps. We call it stress eating. For others, it may be money, sex, power, or internet browsing that is their coping mechanism. I tend to think myself into insomnia and a nagging discontent.

This is the negative side of asking lots of questions.

The positive side is that more and more I find that I know what I want. I am more inclined to try and fail than not try at all, because wondering what would happen if I did try this or attempt that seems more interesting than never trying. Life, then, can function a bit like an experiment and in a real sense, this book is a series of notes and observations in leaning my weight on grace so far.

Each chapter is a different question followed by notes, observations, and stories related to that subject. Because we all think in stories, I use anecdotes and narrative quite often. I hope that this book gets under your skin. Honestly, if it does mess with you, then it's more interesting and even more memorable. I have tried, then, to step quietly into your living space and point some things out.

I have also invited you in to my living space because conversations can lead us to unexpected places. I hope people discuss some of the questions with a friend or with a trusted small group of peers. Feel free to hunt me down and I'll buy the coffee and we can tackle some of the questions together.

I have always found it interesting that when Jesus was brought before Pilate, he said very little. Pilate, on the other hand, asked a few questions. The scene is stunning. In today's social media network, people would be quick to defend themselves or emphatic in their insults of Pilate. Jesus lets the questions linger a bit to anyone

Introduction

who is listening. What is truth? What do the crowd or the religious leaders have against this man? Why are you bringing this carpenter turned preacher to me? What is wrong with you?

Jesus says very little. He gets beaten up pretty badly and still lets the questions linger. So, what would it be like to sit with Jesus for a while and let the questions of this life mess with you? Can you embrace the good news on bad days?

For some who pick this book up, the themes may be too familiar or too religious. If this is too familiar, then I am asking you to think about how you got to this very point. Instead of claiming to know this already, jot down some notes as to how you have answered these questions over the years. How have you changed your mind?

If this is too religious, then I wonder if we're really all that different. I don't think religion is very helpful. We can be religious about reading the morning paper or brushing our teeth. Reconsider, then, what religion actually means. Don't move too quickly to thinking of an institution or of organized religion. Instead, think about the habits and ideas that shape your day-to-day life. What do you want and who do you want to be with?

My formal education involves degrees in English literature, communication/theater studies, theology, international education, organizational change, and leadership studies. I love ideas and I believe that each idea can have a life of its own. I grew up, though, in a small, Midwestern town full of farms and factories. So, I believe ideas should get expressed in relationships and lived out on the street. There are no ivory towers in the middle of corn and soybean fields.

Grace and love need expression to make sense. Eventually, each idea—namely grace and love—loses its allure if withheld from a friend or if absent from a family. This is what I want to explore in these pages. Can some things like sacrificial love make more sense and become more real because we took the time to ask some questions? I hope so. It's how I think we learn best.

1

What Do You Want and Desire?

"Desiring another person is perhaps the most risky endeavor of all."
—Elizabeth Gilbert,
Committed: A Skeptic Makes Peace with Marriage

I DON'T KNOW WHAT you want in life nor do I know who you want in life. I just know that you want something. How do I know? It's a secret. I will reveal a bit more later, but for now just trust me. On what basis should you trust me? Good question. After this is over I will let you make that decision. For now, take my hand and hold on. This will get a bit rough at times. At the end, maybe you and I will be a bit closer or maybe we'll just understand each other for the first time. Either way, this should be a very interesting ride.

My name is on the cover of the book, so enough with introductions. And you're reading this, so enough about trying to impress you. By the way, since you're reading this I am already impressed with you. In fact, part of the secret is this: I want you. Last night, I was strolling through the backyard just thinking about you. Well, I was thinking about you most of the time. You see, I like to go for walks to both fill my head and clear it again. It's a neurotic fitness

A Time to Question Everything

program I designed years ago to keep my brain from turning to mush. Unfortunately, I regularly feed my brain junk, so there's flab starting to form and my cerebellum now has love handles. What kind of junk? Let's take for instance my neighbor's yard.

The Grass is Always Greener

Standing at the neighbor's fence, I ask myself, how do I get that type of grass? In my own yard, brown, dead patches of sun-scorched earth nod at innocent bystanders, a tree stump waits to be carved out, and mulch seems to be simply thrown out around the trees as if innovative high school students grew weary of using toilet paper as a prank. The neighbor's grass remains perfectly green and nicely complemented with various flowers. Whoever mows my lawn hacks the heads off the tops of the blades of grass and cares little about the finished product. The sole reason for cutting the grass is simply to make it shorter. The neighbor's grass seems to be cut by an artist. There are no strays on the sidewalk and no survivors hugging the fences. The neighbor even moves the garden hose when mowing the lawn. I sometimes forget but that doesn't mean I don't deserve a yard that looks as nice or nicer than anyone else's on the street. Just because I hate working with my hands (I am not much of an outdoorsman and I really don't like the summer heat) doesn't mean that I am not entitled to a better home and garden. Okay, I don't really care much for gardening either and if flowers come up, that's great, but if they don't, life goes on. Dandelions seem beautiful in open meadows next to waterfalls with wildflowers strewn about the landscape, so why not let them work their magic in the front yard for all to see?

And so most of the really bad decisions I have made in my life seem to begin by the fence in the back yard looking at other people's property. It's when I am in the back plotting out how to get what I don't yet have that I forget all about the fact that there is a front yard full of weeds, a garage with my car inside, and a house where my wife and children also sleep. Yet, by now, I am in the zone. My eyes have seen the glory of the coming of greener

What Do You Want and Desire?

grass. I even begin to sing as if the saints will come marching in to admire whatever else I acquire someday. In fact, I picture really nice people walking by and admiring me. In my head, I overhear conversations where people wonder how they can be like me.

"He just has everything a person could ever desire," says one man.

"I know. And have you seen his yard? The grass looks like the fairway at Augusta National, not like any yard we have ever seen," concludes another.

Yet, at the back fence, looking at the vast array of possibilities posed by other people and their stuff, my world and everything in it seems incomplete. Some religious men and women call this "coveting," which is simply an archaic way of saying I want what I don't yet have. Let's be at least more realistic about this rather precarious position and talk like normal people. And normal people don't use words like "covet"; they use words like "want," and "desire."

When was the last time you were approached by someone in the shopping mall asking you the following question: "Can I help you find something, or are you just coveting what you don't own?" Do guys talk in the local bar about coveting that hot chick? Do women get together over lunch to discuss their hopes, dreams, and covetousness? I don't think so; that would be far too direct of an approach.

Sophisticated, educated people sneak through back yards admiring the greener grass of unsuspecting neighbors before making the decision that life can't go on without that one precious thing that someone else already owns. And I am an educated person; no one needs to tell me what to do and no one needs to lecture me on society's rights and wrongs. I know I own a Chevy Equinox, but just imagine a six-foot tall, green-eyed, blonde man cruising through town in a black BMW convertible. On any day, that BMW makes most any other car look like a heap of junk. And you know I am right, don't you? You never see the driver of the black convertible lament the fact that the four-door Chevy gets better gas mileage and seems to come fully-loaded at a very reasonable ticket price.

A Time to Question Everything

The owner of a Chevy Equinox, though, could be envied if he lived in a house overlooking the ocean. People may shun the car, but they can't possibly argue with a Jacuzzi tub in the master bath, with a sliding glass door leading out to the balcony from the master bedroom. Salty air soothes the nerves and even the owner of this house can rest easy in a family sedan because the heavy breathing of the ocean whispers good night every day of the week. Who cares about the neighbor's grass when the backyard is Atlantic whitecaps?

Unfortunately, the ocean isn't my backyard at all. Rather it's this insignificant plot of grass that sits only a few feet from my neighbor's sprawling garden. I just learned that pansies aren't really feminine men who avoid beer, trucks, and football. They are actually flowers growing in the neighbors' yard. Sometimes, these meticulous neighbors even show up at church picnics.

And yes, I have been to a church picnic or two. They are like class reunions, if you ask me. Reunions—family, class, or otherwise—seem to be ripe ground for checking out yards. After all, the whole underlying theme of a class reunion is to find out who is doing what, where, and with whom. The class reunion is simply a less sophisticated phrase that describes strolling through backyards. Let's be brutally honest with ourselves. If the class clown reports after ten years that he or she is making a quarter million dollars a year, lives outside Chicago, and has a three-car garage and two kids in private preschools, then we're at least saying to ourselves, "What's wrong with my yard? And why is his grass the color of money?"

The envy of another's yard is not only bothersome, it's also the exhausting amount of time it takes for me to care for my own yard. Experts in the lawn care industry say that we are to mow our lawns to around 3 inches high and to do it frequently. We are also to add fertilizer in the autumn months and water regularly. And, as if this isn't enough responsibility, we are to keep dandelions at a minimum and control the amount of crabgrass that infiltrates our lawns. These outdoor experts must be laughing at the irony of keeping crabgrass away from grumpy people who work long hours and still have the time to complain about Mr. Jones and his exquisite yard overlooking the entrance to the cul-de-sac.

So, not only have I made some rather poor decisions in life while strolling around in the back, admiring other people's grass, I have also neglected to care for the yard that I have been given. I simply don't want to do the work it takes to have a beautiful lawn. I would rather complain about not having the yard next door than to actually do the work necessary to make my own grass flourish. And this is called wanting something I don't yet own. When this desire is given arms and legs, then it's called something else. But, until we act upon whatever we see in the neighbor's yard, it's admiration, envy, or wanting. This desire is the root of everything we hold dear. No one has ever chased down an ugly patch of grass. No, in our mind's eye, the grass is always greener. Always.

Window Shopping

So whose grass have you been looking at today? Okay, maybe you live in the city and there isn't much grass around. You're not thinking about the neighbor's yard because they don't have one. The only grass you see is in a park and the city kindly takes care of mowing all things, paid for with tax dollars. Let me then tell you about another time I was walking. Downtown Chicago is home to some of the most beautiful buildings in the United States. I used to live there for a time, and I miss the skyline overlooking Lake Michigan. I miss Grant Park, the Art Institute, and the walk along the Chicago River.

Strolling down State Street during Christmastime, one can enjoy the window displays that entertain crowds and, for a brief time, creativity outshines the almighty dollar. Taking a right, I stroll toward Michigan Avenue and to a stretch of land known as the "Magnificent Mile." On one beautiful, crowded piece of real estate are dozens of stores that compete for attention. I know a ton of people who simply love to window shop in downtown Chicago. This, of course, fuels this appetite to want things we don't yet have.

A Time to Question Everything

Oh, no one is trying to purchase a window per se, and no one is really shopping if they're simply standing outside the store. This entire scenario isn't anything but wishful thinking or desire. I want something and you want something. We define that wanting with a word—desire—and our desires tend to define us. At least they are the beginning, the foundation of who we are. Every decision we make in life is linked to our desires. I typically don't do things that I don't want to do. And my guess is, neither do you. In fact, most people I know who are not in prison or institutionalized in some capacity act on their desires pretty regularly. So a fundamental question for you and I to establish is this: What do you want? What is it really that you desire?

Wants and Desires

Maybe you want to be filthy rich or maybe you just want a raise at work. Maybe you want to have sex with a certain man or woman or maybe you just want your spouse to give you the time of day. Maybe you want to be noticed at school or maybe you want to disappear for a while. Maybe you want to sleep in a little longer or maybe you want to stay up a little later. And so we go on our way, our wants, our desires aching inside us like labor pains, like a child inside us begging to come out and breathe the air of life. Stop walking with me for a second and take a deep breath. Now, close your eyes. In your mind's eye, can you picture what you desire? Can you see a vision of what you want? Now, come closer and whisper what you see into my ear.

You're hesitating. I see. You want me to go first. Your desires are personal then, aren't they? We're no longer talking about abstract ideas, but something real. Our desires are very real. In fact, your hesitation tells me what I suspected when we first met: you desire something that you not only *don't* have, but something that you probably *shouldn't* have. Your reluctance to whisper what is truly on your mind tells me that you don't want all of your desires to be known. I understand. So, let's not whisper secrets just yet. Just take my hand and walk with me some more. I won't pressure

What Do You Want and Desire?

you because I understand what you're going through. Let's just walk together. Relax, I will go first. And no, I won't whisper in your ear, I will speak plainly.

I want enough money to be able to give some away without really altering my lifestyle. I want to sacrifice, but not too much. I want to be kissed with passion, not with compliance, routine, or a sense of mundane responsibility. I want a woman to kiss me like I am the only human contact she will have for an indeterminable amount of time. I want to be on mission, but on my own time and without the pressure to meet deadlines or pay bills. I want world peace, but I want other people to change first, so that my part in the process is relatively easy. Should I continue? You're nodding, so I will.

I want the church to be more concerned about the poor and downtrodden than about its size and stature. I want the government to be for the people and not just for certain people. I want to read the best books in the English language and regularly visit the cinema and theatre. I want a healthy marriage, healthy children, and a healthy body. I want chocolate chip cookies and a cold glass of milk every afternoon. I want to sleep at night without interruption and I want to dream of beautiful things that make me smile when I wake up. I want patience for long lines and rush-hour traffic and I want peace of mind when the day ends. I want to be forgiven for what I have done wrong and I want to hear someone say "I love you," and believe them. And I want all these things at a young age so I can enjoy them for decades to come.

I'll stop there because I can tell, by the look on your face that you're not used to a lot of transparency when discussing what we really desire. You don't think all of them are ideal do you? You'll question some of them and want to tone down others a bit. This happens way too much in this world. We self-edit far too quickly and way too often.

Instead, we should, like many of the Psalms, just let it all out. What is it that you and I really want? It's hard to repeat this question too often because it frames so many of our days. We typically do what we want to do.

A Time to Question Everything

We also want good things to happen to us. We struggle because the Bible has rules, also called laws, that set limitations on us, and if we're honest, we don't like it. God-given laws are guides and gifts, but in all honesty, if seen apart from grace, these same rules will crush us. We don't keep a single one of them and the guilt or shame is painful without good news. While many of these laws restrain people, all of them reveal us as less than perfect. We don't even like that label either. Who wants to be called a sinner?

"Hey Bob, did you hear about that sinner?" says the man drinking the Heineken.

"Yeah, his sins are terrible," says the bartender.

"How long has he been a sinner?" asks the man.

"For a very long time is what I hear," says the bartender.

The word just sounds bad. Unfortunately, it also makes a lot of sense.

Somewhere during my days in high school, I began to believe, for the first time, that I might be a sinner and that I had actually been a sinner since birth. I was a natural-born sinner, and while I didn't care about singing hymns or about organ music, I did care about being forgiven, if indeed I was a sinner. Unfortunately, another dilemma arose in my life. In addition to learning that I was a sinner, I learned that some people spend eternity in hell, while others spend eternity in heaven. Those particular concepts didn't bother me, because they're not any idea of mine. I am still learning about heaven and its wonder. I am still learning about hell and its separation from all that is good. I wouldn't create a place like heaven or hell because I liked a lot of Earth way too much to think of living elsewhere. My dilemma didn't lie in who went where either, because some people are evil and should go to hell. Other people seem very nice and shouldn't have to spend eternity with the scum of the earth. My dilemma arose with where *I* would spend eternity. I didn't want to go to hell, because that place sounds terrible. Demons, wicked people, fire, gnashing of teeth, and the devil himself occupying the same place without any hope of release or relief sounds awful. I did not and I do not want to go to hell.

What Do You Want and Desire?

But, I didn't want to go to heaven either. Why? Because people going to church were supposed to live in heaven and there were so many people sitting in pews every Sunday morning who made me upset. Greedy, judgmental people sitting together, convinced that heaven was in their future; people who assumed they would get to heaven because they deserved it. And so I began to wander the earth, go for long walks, trying to wrap my brain around what to do. My desire to find answers landed me in the pages of the Bible.

The Bible has shown me something clearly, and it's this: our desires are indeed messy. I am a mess living in a messed up world. So I walk with you, torn by sin and salvation. Each word has wrecked my life. I wanted salvation, but received awareness of sin first. I want to sin, but am reminded of salvation. I want one, but need the other. I want contentment, but receive conviction instead. I want to be Christlike, but instead I am typically conflicted.

I don't know if you think you're a sinner or not, or even if the word makes any sense to you. I do know that you probably have desires, like mine, that aren't always considered, well, right. Whether you sympathize with the liberals or the conservatives, deep down some of your desires are a bit suspect. Well, cheer up, the entire human race struggles with this from birth.

Take, for example, that woman with her two small children standing over there. Do you see the one throwing a tantrum? What is he, about three years old? Now, did that little boy ever watch his parents throw themselves on the ground and scream and cry out loud? I don't think so. He just does that because he isn't getting what he wants. I have heard lots of educated people actually dismiss this as childish behavior. The child is supposed to grow out of this behavior like his mother. But, take a look at her. She's tugging at him, grabbing him, clenching her teeth, and getting very upset with him. If it's just childish behavior, then what's the big deal? Why does the mother care so much if it's only a temporary phase? She cares because she desires obedience without complaint or tantrums. The little boy desires to do whatever he wants and could care less about rules and his mother's moral code at this point. As we watch the interaction, we see that both the boy and

A Time to Question Everything

his mother want something and neither seem to be getting what they so desire.

Hardly anyone I know is satisfied with their life. There's always something that could be better. One writer has said, "We all want to make our plans for life and living."[1] No kidding. The ones who come to the realization that they are indeed discontent are the ones who tend to inspire us. Admitting our own discontent is the beginning of the journey, not the end. Unfortunately, so many people never get started. Paralysis by analysis or some other disease plagues their minds because they can't take a deep breath and admit that they might be a sinner. Just maybe some of the discontentment in the world is linked to desires that should be held in check or thrown out altogether. Then again, maybe our problem isn't our desires, but our unwillingness to act them out. Everything in the core of our being desires something, but for some reason, we just sit and do nothing. No wonder the advertising world is loaded with commercials asking if we're depressed or unhappy with life. At least the pharmaceutical sales teams understand something about humanity that much of the church wants to ignore: namely, the vast majority of us desire something we don't have and we desire to be different than who we are.

Churches rush too quickly to talk about sharing faith, becoming preachers, or signing up for the mission trip overseas. No one can do these things without first admitting that their desires are unfulfilled. Every pew-sitter on the planet wants something to be different either in the world or in the church, otherwise the church would be more mobilized than it is stagnant.

Have you ever noticed that Jesus seems to be totally satisfied with his religion and so many of his followers seem disappointed with theirs? Jesus seems perfectly content with God, while his followers seem to argue incessantly about the teachings of their God and then, which shouldn't surprise us, struggle to have faith in that same God.

So here we are walking together, wanting something. I don't know what you want, but you know at least a bit of what I want.

---

1. Lloyd-Jones, *Let Not Your Hearts Be Troubled*, 17.

What Do You Want and Desire?

And this is only the beginning of our walk together. For this walk to be successful or useful, we're going to have to remind each other to stop and be a bit more observant than usual. Yes, we should smell the roses, but we should also see the thorns, the green stem, and the petals waving in the wind. We need open hearts and open eyes.

Have you ever seen a painting by Jackson Pollack? If you have not, then you should know that what's fascinating is not so much his subject matter, but his technique. It's been well documented. Pollack would put the canvas on the floor, walk around it, drip paint, splashing here and drizzling there, becoming part of the artwork himself. To many, he was a master of his craft, but to the distant observer his paintings look like a total mess. In other words, Pollack's paintings make far more sense when entering into them than they do from a distance. As with so many works of art, the more personal they can become, the bigger the impact they will have.

And this is why I must tell you something important. I invite you to walk with me, but from here, the path we're on must be taken personally and cannot be watched from a distance. This is a path that doesn't go farther until it is taken deeper and more seriously, for such is the path that stands the test of time. If we're both willing to meet a God who is different than us, whose thoughts are higher than any human, whose sense of fairness and whose idea of love is intense and countercultural, then we should wrestle with our own deep questions. There is no other way.

Blaming other people will not get you the answers you want. Avoiding all the bad people will not move you toward a deeper understanding of love and grace. You will not find peace without exploring the desires of your heart.

2

Am I the Problem?

> "He'd redefine the problem or the approach
> and our little problem would go away."
>
> —Walter Isaacson writing on Steve Jobs

SCANDALS ON COLLEGE CAMPUSES, mysterious strains of new diseases or unknown viruses, and the ongoing threat of nuclear war seem to be part of the evening news with numbing regularity. Children still go hungry, AIDS still has no cure, and shootings in American schools happen with painful and shocking frequency. Let's not gloss over the hateful rhetoric spewed over various channels by political leaders and their constituencies. It's so easy to point fingers nowadays and social media allows us to lob vitriol from a distance, naming everything and everyone else as the problem. And as the days turn into months and the months turn into years, the division and gridlock oozes into our daily life and suddenly, without warning, we've grown used to living in a culture that outlaws hate crimes, but whose leaders at the highest level participate in hateful language demonizing opponents wherever a political advantage can be found. The toxic nature of hate-filled language

Am I the Problem?

and postures of blame encourages us to distance ourselves from those who think differently than we do. Suddenly, we've become masters at identifying the problem.

It's rarely you and it's rarely me.

Let's explore something different. Let's call a time out and press pause.

What happens if I truly seek to discover the sobering truth? What if I am part of the problem?

I am white, I attend a local church, and I am the son of hard-working, blue-collar laborers who did not attend college. All of these attributes get unfairly lumped into a particular camp without any thought to nuance or the negligence of such generalizations. I did not vote for Donald Trump. Yet polling that generalizes "white evangelicals" who watch Fox News and who get public ridicule for the rise of men like Trump has got me thinking. I don't really belong in the conservative Republican camp, nor do I completely feel like I can drink the Kool-Aid on the progressive Democrat side either. Is there room for a center viewpoint? Can someone, like me, refuse to be completely cornered by the right or the left?

What this means is that I feel rather homeless, politically. Almost every media news outlet has run stories decrying the white male and the white male vote and in so many words saying that white males are responsible for Donald Trump's victory in November of 2016. Yet, while I am white (heck, my last name is even White), I am not sure what camp is my home. I do not carry a gun. I am not a fan of the death penalty. I believe that a pro-life, "womb to tomb" stance is both proper and life affirming. I am college educated, but do not believe that college should be free or mandatory. I think such discussions overlook or make less of the hard-working people I grew up around who rather enjoyed working on a farm or who simply wanted to live a simple life.

Yet, on November 9, 2016, *The Washington Post* printed these words online: "White evangelicals are the religious group that most identifies with the Republican Party," and later on, a tweet was quoted that read: "America will never forget the 80%

A Time to Question Everything

of evangelicals who voted for Trump."[1] In a January 2016 article entitled, "What is White Privilege?" Christine Emba helpfully provides this definition,

> White privilege is something specific and different—it's the idea that by virtue of being a white person of any kind, you're part of the dominant group which tends to be respected, assumed the best of, and given the benefit of the doubt.[2]

I admit I get defensive at the idea of white privilege because I didn't grow up with much money, yet what trips me up is not the idea of privilege, but the phrase "dominant group." This connotes power and seems to say that privilege isn't economic (though it can be), but this term is actually being linked to a group that can take certain things for granted. Having traveled all over the world, I truly believe that the U. S. as a whole takes its privileges for granted and I do believe that "privilege" is a layered term that has both individual and systemic consequences if properly explored and unpacked. Yet the times we live in demand self-awareness and self-reflection. We should be sobered by the way we live. We don't steward privilege, wealth, and abundance of choice all that well.

As someone who embraces grace as it's articulated in the teachings of Jesus, I don't resonate with the evangelicals who promote fear or dislike of anyone who disagrees with them. I am fallible, imperfect, and prone to wander from that which is good, true, and beautiful. I know this all too well. So the ideological lines that have been drawn do not always describe me very well.

I think it's okay to change your mind. The Bible calls this repentance; Alcoholics Anonymous calls it recovery. Yet in the past several years people who change their mind are beaten up publicly with vile words and one would think that flip-flopping is the unpardonable sin. Didn't you use to believe in slavery or were you raised by a racist? Then you'll always be a bigot. Didn't you once have an abortion? Then you're a criminal. Did you vote

---

1. Pulliam Bailey, "White Evangelicals Voted," lines 8–9.
2. Emba, "What is White Privilege?" para. 5.

Am I the Problem?

for a Democrat or a Republican? Then you're either a backwards conservative or a dangerous liberal.

I believe with all my heart that we all can make a positive difference in the world. And I believe with all my heart that I am still part of the problem, but perhaps not in the way the media or internet claims. Organized protests and marches only motivate me for a few weeks or months and then I am back to having to deal with myself. At some point I must deal with my own junk even if I sit in, speak out, or stand up for what is right. Even if I am publicly on the right side of an issue, the command to love drives me into relationship with my opponents and to not simply lob words or tweets from a distance.

Am I privileged? Yes. I am humbled and grateful for gifts in the form of education, travel, and networks of friends and family. Am I living in poverty? No. While it's true that I have lived below the poverty line in the past and I have seen extreme poverty around the world, I do not currently live day to day wondering how I will eat or where I will sleep. Most of the activists I know personally and professionally are also not poor. And hardly anyone I know wants to be poor. I live among people who have been given much. Am I aware of the prejudice and harm that white males have perpetuated over the years? Yes. From the treatment of Native Americans to the treatment of African-Americans to the lack of equal pay for women to a whole range of other issues, white males have participated in some oppressive and life-sucking stuff. Yet, while these issues trigger some kind of personal reaction, this isn't why I am part of the problem.

I am part of the problem because I do things I shouldn't do, and I leave undone things I should do. *The Book of Common Prayer* guides its readers with this confession:

> Most merciful God, we confess that we have sinned against you in thought, word, and deed, by what we have done, and by what we have left undone. We have not loved you with our whole heart; we have not loved

A Time to Question Everything

our neighbors as ourselves. We are truly sorry and we humbly repent.[3]

I don't get to say things like, "I have sinned in thought, word, and deed, but I am not as bad as those other people who are unloving, uneducated, and unenlightened." I also don't get to say, "I have loved you with my whole heart and my neighbor as myself, except for those neighbors who see the world differently than me." I am part of the problem because the overflow of my heart results in some kind of activity or action. I am part of the problem because the overflow of my heart also results in some kind of inertia that is selfish and sometimes I am even self-protective. And this conflict of inertia and self-interested movement is what I want to explore further because it's this that causes me to wake up to the good news and bad days. I need to deal with the tension of my misguided laziness, but I also need to deal with my willingness to act out in any way I like—both sides have been harmful to people who I claim to love.

Piano Lessons as an Adult

One of the best gifts I have ever received for my birthday or any other celebration was a certificate for eight weeks of piano lessons. I have always wanted to take up an instrument but was unable to do this as a child. So, while I was in graduate school for theological studies, I showed up at a rather nice old lady's house for eight straight weeks to learn the basics of playing piano. I loved it.

The only troubling part was that my teacher wanted to talk about what I was studying which sometimes cut into the amount of time we had for instruction.

"Do you really think that the study of God—if there is one—is helpful?" she would ask.

"I don't think I am wasting my time searching for answers, if that's what you are asking," I always replied.

---

3. *Book of Common Prayer*, 79.

Am I the Problem?

Then she would turn me back to the lesson and try to get me to put my hands on the keys properly.

"You know what the problem is with most adults?" she said one day.

"No, I guess I don't," I replied.

"Shortcuts! Adults want to know the shortcut. You see, to truly master an instrument, you first need to learn where to put your hands. Whether it's the guitar or the piano or the drum, you can't just show up and put your hands wherever you feel like. Then you have to learn the notes and learn to read the music and all of this takes time. Most adults, though, just want to learn how to play songs and there's a word for that," she said.

"And what's the word?" I asked.

"Cheating," she said without looking up from the sheet music.

I still do not know how to play an instrument the way I want to or in a way that can produce a recognizable song, but I do remember some things my piano teacher taught me, like the lesson that adults often take shortcuts. We want to jump quickly to performances without learning to read the notes or hand positions. In other words, we don't do as we ought and we run quickly to that which we should not do.

I think the Christian life, or a life that is characterized by grace, is one that takes time. Running straight to performance without being able to understand the music is, in a word, cheating.

I am not sure I want to learn what I need to learn in order to play the music of grace properly. So I may cheat and hope that some politician can create a better environment around me. I may cheat and hope that someone else takes the first step toward me and calls me their friend. I may cheat and hope that poverty is solved through legislation, even though I know that anything of lasting value happens in the context of a healthy relationship.

The headlines about white men and their oppressive ways hurt me and my heart aches at the sweeping assumptions being made all over Western culture. Protesting, though, has seemed to me to be a tactic that must be sustained, focused, and planned. Successful protests involve sacrifice and more time than mere

A Time to Question Everything

words. We don't just get to complain with other people and do nothing else. Our sense of what is right and what is good leads us to move toward something better. And sacrifice involves a bit of personal reflection and soul searching because we can't sacrifice ourselves for just anything.

Questions Rooted in Grace

I am haunted at times by the words of Dr. Martin Luther King, Jr., in his "Letter from a Birmingham Jail" where he speaks of being "gravely disappointed with the white moderate."[4] I have an audio book version of Dr. King's letter and I listen to it in the car every so often. It's less than an hour and the copy I have is read by Dion Graham. It's sometimes hard to listen to and on one occasion I had to pull the car over because I couldn't see through my own tears. Yet, I think it's part of the music I need to learn in order to understand grace well. I think it's part of the notes I need to practice before I seek to perform a song.

I am aware, though, that learning can sometimes be an excuse to not take action. So part of my story is that grace isn't easy and living a life marked by grace is hard. We live in a world that rewards top performers, so grace isn't even encouraged as much as individual performance. I even judge *me* on the basis of performance and I don't live up to my own standards at times. I don't always show up to meetings on time and I don't always return library books on the due dates. I need grace as a way of life because breaking rules is a way of life. Do rules matter? Yes. But, because we are all breakers of even our own rules, grace truly makes an incredible difference.

So what follows in this book is a series of questions where I am trying to learn the music. I battle melancholy at times and have even put myself in the hospital because of depression (more on that soon). I sometimes fight loneliness, though I have been extremely blessed with friends and family.

---

4. Brown, "Martin Luther King's Scorn," para. 7.

Am I the Problem?

I don't understand why some social issues are immediate headlines while others hardly get any attention at all. I don't understand why I can get really worked up about making the world better on one day and then binge watch "Mozart in the Jungle," the next day. I wonder if you relate, and if so, then this is an invitation to walk with me in these pages and reflect on your own life and your own rules. I believe that grace actually allows us to question everything. Yes, at some point you and I need to decide where we stand on things, but our stance becomes stronger with personal inspection. That's right, I said inspection.

If you buy a house, you pay for an inspection to be done and a professional comes and looks for cracks in the foundation or termites or structural dangers and defects. We can afford to do the same with our own lives and our own hearts. Are there structural flaws that need attention in my own heart?

I am part of the problem. I *actually am* part of the problem.

And what's sobering is that it's much worse than *The Washington Post* or *The New York Times* reports. After all, most reports evaluate the performance without first exploring how adults take shortcuts in the first place.

Living at the speed of redemption is both heartbreaking and heartwarming. We are traveling as fast as sacrificial love moves us. In Ecclesiastes 3:1, we read that "for everything there is a season and a time for every matter under heaven," which reminds us that these seasons reveal not only what life throws at us, but also how we are wired to respond. Zack Eswine adds that

> The result is that we try to force others to act or the world to exist within the confines of the handful of seasons that we are most comfortable with. We try to control others to stay within the seasonal behaviors that we most prefer rather than learn how to change and to adjust teachably, slowly, and adequately."[5]

---

5. Eswine, *Recovering Eden*, 130.

A Time to Question Everything

Eswine is also helpful when he states that "we need the grace therefore to relate teachably toward each day that we have been given."[6]

Each day we may find ourselves asking questions of the messy life we live, and day by day we will need to rely on the fact that grace can hold the weight of whatever answers come our way. Instead of asking someone if they are saved or if he or she believes a certain doctrine or agrees with a certain camp, I think it would be fun to simply ask this question: Are you ready to live a life that purposely enters in to the mess you helped make?

---

6. Ibid., 125.

3

Do You Want to Live or Die?

"So instead of giving in to despair I chose active melancholy, in so far as I was capable...."

—Vincent Van Gogh, *Letter to Theo, July 1880*

"Do you want to die?" he asked.

"I wouldn't mind going to sleep and not waking up," I replied.

I can't remember if I wanted to commit suicide or just get some sleep. Swallowing nearly twenty pills, though, did qualify as excessive. After being rushed to the emergency room, I remember lying half-awake in an overdosed stupor. The resident psychiatrist began asking a series of diagnostic questions. I remember only the one.

A few details, I suppose, are worth mentioning. I did not go into the bathroom and slam a bottle of pills. Instead, I spent almost a week not being able to sleep. Of course, this inability to sleep was preceded by several months of anxiety, depression, and unchecked stress. This led to all kinds of issues when the time to go to bed actually came. Preparing for bed included brushing teeth and navigating a mental fog followed by sleepless hours punctuated by

A Time to Question Everything

increased stress. One day, I had enough of that futility and took some over-the-counter sleeping aid, a few pills at a time, over a couple hours. I just kept taking the pills; the stupid things didn't seem to work. So, I just kept taking them until the damn things helped me sleep. My inner turmoil caught up with my external needs and I crashed. I just wanted a break from this world.

I am told that the ER visit lasted several hours. The IV going into my arm, the bland color of the room, and that one question remain my only memories of a rather horrible day. Prior to the overdose, everything in life seemed very dark. Emotionally, my heart seemed like the site of a train wreck, tracks leading everywhere with pieces littered all around. Physically, I had been experiencing consistent fatigue and exhaustion. I was not taking days off. I was not happy at home. I was not spending much time with friends. I was struggling with advice given to me by friends and different counselors. I just wanted a break. I just wanted to go to sleep.

After the overdose, I began a regimen of visits to counselors and psychiatrists. This came with a flurry of experimental antidepressants prescribed by professionals who wanted me to feel better. The drugs made me feel worse. In fact, I can't remember ever feeling any closer to death. Maybe not physical death, but the utter burial of anything I held dear in daily life. The desire for intimacy, food, exercise, and creativity vanished overnight with these amazing little pills. Frustrated and exhausted, I tried whatever I could to find some kind of rest. I stumbled through life in a stupor most of the time. I didn't like who I was becoming or how I was feeling. I concluded that I would rather feel my life ebb away than be numbed by any prescription drug. I quit any drug labeled antidepressant. Let me stress that this does not mean antidepressants don't work. In fact, some friends have had some positive experiences with antidepressant medication. My body didn't react that well to them, so I made a change.

This was not an easy decision at the time. No major Plan B existed. All I had was learning how to put one foot in front of the other and walking slowly toward something better.

Eventually, I found a counselor who created a safe space for healing conversation and exploration. We explored past trauma, current questions, and future habits. We talked about how I got to the place where sleep itself was hard to find. There are research studies that demonstrate how we need sleep just to retain sanity. The first step in this entire process was to be honest with myself and the counselor. I credit the counselor with getting this out of me. I finally was able to say out loud "I am not doing well."

Ah, but this was only the beginning.

Following Adam and Eve

The writer of Ecclesiastes uses the words "meaningless" or "vanity" to describe life under the sun. It's a toilsome series of events that seems cursed. And in a sense this echoes the exile from Eden when Adam and Eve were told that their work would change from being delightful to discouraging. After the proverbial original sin, I wonder when Adam lay down at night next to Eve, if they ever were naked on top of the sheets, facing each other with expressions of exhaustion instead of exclamation?

I wonder what it was like the first time he bit into a piece of fruit. Did he spit it out immediately or chew slowly? I think maybe he did both. As the memory followed Adam out of the garden of Eden, he might have tossed and turned at night until he couldn't take it any longer. Maybe he looked at his wife and cursed under his breath hearing the words, "it is not good for man to be alone," echo in his mind. What was it like the first time he stepped on a thistle and cut his foot open? I would presume that Adam must have recalled something positive in his mind otherwise he couldn't have possibly found sleep. After all, it was when he awoke from a deep sleep that the woman first appeared. Did he ever wake up again and wish she was suddenly gone? Then again, did his mind ever venture to that place before he fell asleep and remember the rest that once was his? Did his mind ever wish to simply go home?

I recall one night a few years ago when I couldn't sleep at all. It was a few months after the ER visit, so I was supposedly on the

A Time to Question Everything

mend. Rubbing my eyes, I stumbled into the bathroom. I didn't want to wake up my wife, so I tried to urinate in the dark. I was judging my aim by the sound of water flowing into the toilet. Any man who has attempted this little challenge has met with both victory and defeat. On this particular evening, I was defeated. Since I felt low anyway, and since I was struggling to find any peace of mind, I didn't bother to clean up whatever spillage dripped onto the floor. Instead, I sat down and began to cry.

Curling up on the floor, like a little child who wants to be held, I simply wept as quietly as possible. This was one of those long-awaited Kleenex marathons spilling out from a sadness held deep within the secret places of the heart. The cry was like brushing dust off of old family photographs, allowing me to remember clearly that I may not be alone. Peeling myself up off the floor, I tiptoed back to bed, pleased that no one else was awake, but dejected because that meant no one else was going to hold me and tell me that everything will turn out all right. Nonetheless, the tears washed some emotional grime and dirt away which is no small thing when it comes to interior cleansing. Strangely, the private humiliation on the floor in the bathroom surprised me and, more strangely, it warmed my heart.

There is a sense that only when one is in darkness does one search for the light. Whether it was a psychosis, epiphany, turning point, or simply a wake-up call, the cry in the bathroom remains an oddly-treasured memory. Tears washed away the blindness that prevented me from seeing any light at all. I suppose this is labeled depression in modern clinical terms, but Lamentations 3 seems to capture the complexity and spirituality of the moment. In it Jeremiah writes, "He has driven me away and made me walk in darkness rather than light" (3:2), and "Even when I call out or cry for help, he shuts out my prayer" (3:8). But the passage doesn't end with such words. "Because of the Lord's great love, we are not consumed, for his compassions never fail. They are new every morning; great is your faithfulness" (3:22–23). While it is good to cry out in darkness, "it is good to wait quietly for the salvation of the Lord" (3:25) as well. And it seems to me that the Lord God isn't in any hurry whatsoever. So, I wait and wait and trust that salvation is a reality.

Maybe you can identify with feeling alone or feeling like God is distant. If so, then understand that not only are you truly human, but you may be closer to the light you desire to find than you realize. Lights shine brighter and function better when it's dark. Amidst the darkness our search truly begins. Jesus said, "Blessed are you who hunger and thirst for righteousness" (Matt 5:6), but this is a difficult idea in a culture obsessed with being full. We want to eat all we can and we will create drinks that quench thirst. Likewise, when there are cities that never sleep and have lights that never seem to go off, we may struggle simply because we no longer search for answers to the deep questions of life. In short, the darkness is sometimes necessary to experience, so that we may truly find real light.

Lighting Up at Church

I trudged into church week after week amidst a cloud of depression, haunting sense of failure, and exhaustion. This was more work than I originally suspected. Singing songs of joy is difficult when the doctor says that I am on the verge of losing my mind. On one Sunday morning, though, I began to see things differently. In the middle of a sermon, my mind wandered and, while this happens a lot nowadays due to so many preachers being full of information and rather short on inspiration, this day was different. Instead of thinking about my to-do list or the wretched-looking dress of that one lady sitting across from me, instead of looking at all of the bored teenagers and their disinterested parents, I thought to myself, what would happen if I lit up a cigarette right here, right now?

There is no explicit rule against smoking in church, at least not in the Bible. I can picture the ushers coming forward with ash trays, passing them like the offering plate, and I calmly tap my cigarette on them, taking in a drag or two as the preacher drones on. I also can see the ushers being summoned by some well-meaning

A Time to Question Everything

members of the congregation. A man, elbowed by his wife, stands up, whispers into the ear of one of the ushers, and points at me. I can see the man pointing, but I simply and silently puff on the cigarette and exhale a ring of smoke into the air. The ring quickly dissipates as the ushers lead me out of the service.

Once outside, I politely drop the cigarette to the ground and smother it, twisting my foot just to make sure it's out. And then, I walk away from the church. I keep walking, searching for a place to call home. At one point, I stop, turn around, and yell back at the church building: "What about the old man who fell asleep in front of me? Why does he get to stay?"

I receive no response, so I keep walking, and yes, my mind can wander while sitting in church. Snapping back to reality, I hear the preacher coming to his conclusion. The message has the familiar tone of advice and good counsel, but it lacks something. It's an agreeable message, but no emotion is stirred. I am simply sitting in church, mouthing words and wondering if everyone around me truly believes this stuff.

Susanna Kaysen strangely encourages me when she writes,

> I think melancholy is useful. In its aspect of pensive reflection or contemplation, it's the source of many books (even those complaining about it) and paintings, much scientific insight, the resolution of many fights between couples and friends, and the process known as becoming mature. Here are the characteristic feelings: It's all wrong. I did it wrong. I'm no good at this. This idea stinks. That paragraph doesn't mean anything. These data don't add up to squat. We always end up yelling about the same two things. I can't ever seem to bring anything I start to completion. Next step: why bother?[1]

Why bother with church? Why bother with religion? Why does Jesus bother me so much? I don't mean bother as in he annoys me, but I mean consistent interruption. Jesus consistently interrupts my life and I wonder why he bothers with someone like me at all. David was the King of Israel when he wrote many of

---

1. Kaysen, "One Cheer for Melancholy," 39.

the Psalms. Job was described as "blameless and upright, one who feared God and turned away from evil" (Job 1:1). I am often depressed, detached, and prone to wander. Jesus, though, still bothers me, interrupts me, and bugs me. Jesus seems just as interested in me when I am down and out as he does when I am fully engaged in ministry and liking it. And that's the part of Jesus that seems a bit insane. In fact, when I am poor in spirit, Jesus seems strikingly clear.

Church is the only group where membership requires me to confess my utter depravity. Church goes a step further than Alcoholics Anonymous or other support groups where I *only* have to agree with confessing alcoholism. Christianity requires me to admit more than alcoholism; it also requires me to admit self-absorption, idolatry, lust, hatred, jealousy, laziness, falsehood, and my disregard of authority. In other words, desperation and helplessness meets grace in AA, Christianity, and in loving relationships. Yet, we so often avoid these communities because we truly want to prove ourselves to each other and to the world.

Jesus, then, calls the church his betrothed or bride. The wedding feast described at the end of the Bible begins with the love of a pursuing Jesus found in Genesis 3 at the beginning of the Bible. This doesn't make sense. But you know what else doesn't make sense? Me. And if I am brutally honest, you don't make sense either. I mean seriously, look at us. Look at our confusion mixed in with our confession of faith and our weak convictions mixed together with our conflicted hearts and convoluted minds. Look at us mouth the words to songs during church services and on the way home mouth curses at the driver ahead of us. Look at us glare at our children as if they were somehow more sinful than we are or have been.

Every Christian story—that is, every Christian's testimony—begins with trusting in a man who is described with the following words: "He was despised and rejected by men; a man of sorrows and acquainted with grief; and as one from whom men hide their faces, he was despised, and we esteemed him not" (Isa 53:3). We can call faith and grace countercultural or counterintuitive, but the

A Time to Question Everything

bottom line is this: to the rest of the world, this way of life, where we embrace our desperate search for love and acceptance, doesn't always make much sense.

For some of you, insomnia is not your issue. You may stress eat or binge drink. You may numb out in front of your favorite electronic device. You may carry around an undercurrent of anger. All of us have ways we are using to cope with our lack of measuring up to the standards of God or even the standards of our own self-made universe. Sometimes we just want to know deeply that there is light at the end of the tunnels we're walking through.

Is this Jesus or this gospel really the hope of the entire world?

4

Should We Fit In or Find Out?

> "It's not a silly question if you can't answer it."
> —Jostein Gaarder, *Sophie's World*

"What about all the other gods in the world? How can you follow only one and ignore the rest?" asked a friend outside a Buddhist temple in China. My response surprised me when I heard my own words out loud.

"Who says I haven't considered the other ones?" I said.

He motioned for me to follow and we walked inside a sacred shrine where he prayed and where I prayed. Incense burned and the adorned temple was far more peaceful and colorful than most churches I had been inside. And to this day I am not sure which god he prayed to nor if I prayed anything intelligent. I do know that we sat side by side in silence for several minutes. Afterward, we found a place to have tea and continue our conversation.

Many aspects of Buddhism appeal to me. And I do think it's worth noting that the flavor of Buddhism that is popular in some parts of the U. S. and Western Europe are not exactly the same as some practiced in Asia. Mindfulness is important and

A Time to Question Everything

so is enlightenment, but deities and the afterlife don't get near as much attention in the West. Over tea, in Southern China, my conversation partner modeled well a listening ear and compassionate space. He didn't sugarcoat suffering and showed great interest in my questions and answers. The issue that we both wrestle with is that, as Richard Wright put it, "attaining our desires always leaves us unsatisfied, thirsting for more of the same or thirsting for something new."[1]

We participate in a recreation of this world. New creation is what artists invite us to, and as some people seek to avoid the idea of spirituality and its connection with reality, I must wonder why. Has this happened to you? Do you avoid spiritual conversation? At what point did you lose your curiosity about spiritual things? This is the question I have asked several dozen adults and the answer is almost always the same.

"You just don't understand. . .God isn't who I thought," he or she says.

Their honesty is supposed to be authentic, but it's not. The preference for what can be seen and proven and believed *if only* tied to science is often an excuse. It's actually a confession that he or she has lost interest in God or in the Bible, and long before I asked the question. Part of it lies in the instant communication culture we currently live in; part of it lies in the way we as human beings settle for shallow answers. The point is this: it's almost impossible to get good answers to bad questions. More than that, it's deeply unsatisfying to get answers to questions you may not be asking at all. Yet, at some point, many men and women simply stop asking deeper questions and move on to more comfortable and pragmatic things.

And this isn't just with God.

When's the last time you found your best friend, your spouse, your family, or your job interesting enough to go deeper into what makes it or him or her or them tick? Have you already settled in to the routine or do you really know how your friend's day has been

---

1. Wright, *Why Buddhism is True*, 209.

going? Do you know what your child's dreams are? What makes people who are not you happy?

Now, this curiosity isn't to satisfy your boredom, rather it's simply to reveal whether or not you're still interested enough to investigate more than those people who say they don't believe. Are you bored with your friends? Are you tired with your lover? And perhaps there's the more uncomfortable question: Are you still interested in that which you say is most important to you?

Types of Questions

In journalism, the ability to ask good questions is essential and great interviewers can lead a person to a narrower and interesting subject. While this is one way to ask questions, this is not what I am talking about. I am talking about old-fashioned care and curiosity instead of boredom and apathy. I am not talking about a trap or the infamous "gotcha" question made famous by Sarah Palin and subsequent comedians and politicians. We're not looking for information either. Those are factual questions, and in the age of the expanding internet those are hardly investigative. In fact, most people will now google their question to see what comes up and then the most popular answers will get listed first. Perhaps you've been guilty of logging on to WebMD prior to seeing a doctor and then you're suddenly ready to disagree with a man or woman who has devoted years and years of their life to the study of the human body.

The Socratic method, used by many universities and graduate schools, may also be a type of questioning, but again, it's typically an interrogation of a thesis, not an investigative exploration of something out of love. In other words, Socrates would make an assertion, state an answer, and then the students would question it from different angles, testing the truth of the statement. And while this is very common, it's not what I mean by curiosity.

I don't mean the curiosity you may have when you are driving down a highway and you slow down to have a good hard look when you see a truck tipped over on its side. Some people call this a "morbid curiosity," while others call it "rubbernecking." A German word, "schadenfreude," means that we get something positive from the bad things that happen to other people. While all these are forms of curiosity, I mean something more.

Jesus says it this way: "Ask and it will be given to you, seek and you will find" (Matt 7:7). The writer of Hebrews clarifies and focuses our curiosity: "without faith it is impossible to please him, for whoever would draw near to God must believe that he exists and that he rewards those who seek him" (Heb 11:6).

Jesus teaches in John's Gospel that we can ask for anything in prayer and receive. In James, we are told to ask when we lack wisdom and to ask when we desire something in prayer. So, why do so many people stop asking Jesus questions or stop seeking to understand a God who is so much bigger than we can imagine?

The answer is simply this: even the things we love can struggle to hold our interest at times because we truly may be trying to fit in more than we are trying to find out. We want to be told what we should believe more than find out who God is. Like an insecure test taker who sneaks a peak at a classmate's answer sheet, we just want to repeat the right answers and get the good marks. We may even want to be content with shallow answers because we are afraid of what we will find out about ourselves as well. What if I am not that interesting? What happens if I am the one who is no longer holding the interest of a loved one, or worse, what if I just want to engage with spiritual things at the same level as the one driving by the church on the way to his son's soccer match? I just grew up attending church and now I don't know why I still go. Am I just afraid of what people will think if I stop?

Fit In or Find Out?

During college, attendance of mid-week chapel services was optional, so the turnout was never huge. Sometimes it felt like a small group while, at other times, during seasonal or special events, the diverse turnout was surprising. During Desert Storm, for example, people could come in to read their Koran or their Bible or simply

Should We Fit In or Find Out?

meditate on a poem as the campus prayed for peace in the Middle East.

On one occasion, I came to chapel about ten minutes late. The day was not going well, and when I arrived I was out of breath from running. When I walked in, the homily was just beginning. Not wanting to interrupt, I found a pew and laid down. Yes, I laid down. Why? To this day, the only reason I could give was that I was tired.

Afterward, others came up to me and wondered what I was doing.

"Why didn't you sit where you normally sit?" asked one person.

"That was a selfish and disruptive thing to do," said another.

"If you were so late, why come at all?" said yet another.

I just wanted to hear more about what the teacher was saying. That's all. I had no desire to be disruptive or even be noticed. And at this point, I figured that God, if there was one and if he created you, me, the heavens, and the earth, didn't care if I sat up, knelt, or collapsed in a heap. I wasn't there to fit in; I was there to find out more about God, myself, and others.

Fitting in, though, is a big fat deal in our world.

When my children were smaller, it took a long time to walk anywhere. Why? Because my son or daughter would find something in the grass and if they found it, then we had to look. We had to stop and then after stopping, we had to talk.

"Daddy, why does this flower fall apart?" one would say about the dandelion.

"Daddy, can we take this stick home? It makes a great sword."

"Daddy, do you know how to blow a whistle with the grass?"

My kids could care less what onlookers were wondering. The ground was just too interesting and it didn't matter that we were on our hands and knees looking at it. Now, what do you do with the ones you love like the God of the Bible? When's the last time you got muddy trying to get a closer look?

To get closer to some mysteries, I have traveled to over forty countries in the world and have studied abroad, taught abroad, worked abroad, and remained connected to international work. I know I am not the center of the world and I am interested in finding out more and more about how people tick.

When the world seems so jacked up that even people seem too hard to deal with, I fight depression, eat too much junk, and struggle to sleep well. I know that there's more to what's in front of me, but sometimes I numb out or check out or simply want out. Sometimes I am afraid that I already know the answer and I'm the one who's disappointing the people I love.

Back in high school, I had a chance to be heroic at least in sports and at least for one night. With one second left on the clock, I had two free throws to either tie or win the game. A teammate had missed a jump shot and I got the rebound and was fouled on the follow up. My coach was encouraging, my teammates were nervous, and I felt pretty much everything at once. I had made dozens of these shots in practice, so this wasn't new. I could do this.

But I didn't do it.

I missed both shots.

And what's the most memorable emotion I felt?

I was not sad or angry or dejected. I was embarrassed—of myself. I was ashamed to be seen.

After standing at the free throw line by myself in front of family and friends, I wanted to vanish. People tried to make me feel better by saying things like, "everyone makes mistakes," or "you'll get 'em next time." I did NOT want to be like everyone who had missed a shot; I wanted to be the one that made the game-winner. It's only a game, you may say, but I will respectfully respond with this: What does that mean to a high school student?

Since then, I have worn a pager as a researcher at a law firm in England and have been in leadership positions where I am tasked with being the primary one on call in regard to crisis response. I have received phone calls where people on the other end of the line have been arrested, beaten, sexually assaulted, robbed, or have called to tell me that I now have to make a phone call to parents, telling them that their son or daughter has died. I have learned to handle pressure better than I handled that miserable free throw shot back in high school.

I have learned that life can throw curve balls and that sometimes things are just plain difficult. I know we don't have this life figured out, which makes me all the more curious as to why people settle for clichés when there's a God who will actually respond? Don't get me wrong, I am not looking for dirty laundry to hang out on every street, but we can do better than "I can't believe in a God that allows bad things to happen." Really? Who gets the easy way out in this life?

Ultimately, though, I don't want pat answers or for people to be fake to my face. I want to know why people do what they do. I want to know what Jesus is really like. I don't just want to fit in, I want to find out.

5

Who Did You Notice Today?

> "And yet in our world everybody thinks of changing humanity, and nobody thinks of changing himself."
>
> —*Leo Tolstoy, Three Methods of Reform*

When I was a student in London, I went looking for adventure with a friend in Amsterdam, but I didn't find what I expected. We were embarking on a two-week backpack trip around Europe and decided to stop in the Netherlands, not only to visit friends, but to take in the sites as well. My mother's maiden name is Huizenga, so the Dutch lineage in my own blood also motivated me to soak in as much as I could while in the land of my ancestors.

We arrived in Amsterdam by train and began to walk the streets. Out of curiosity, we managed to find our way to the Red Light District where anything goes. Prostitution is legal, sex shows abound, and women tap on shop windows wearing next to nothing, offering to do next to anything. It is one of the oldest parts of the city and Old Church remains an architectural beauty amidst drug addicts, peep shows, and sex clubs. This small section of a rather large city is often crowded by the corrupt and the curious.

Who Did You Notice Today?

On this day, I was curious and while we only passed through the Red Light District on the way to another part of town, the lack of restraint exhibited among its clientele remains a vivid image. I reread my journal from that trip and here is a brief note on the Red Light District:

> The canals in Amsterdam are beautiful, but I wonder where the paths and walkways lead. I wonder because we were in the city only a short time and were offered recreational drugs a few times and were a bit startled at the number of sex shops. Explicit only begins to describe them. Down one road is beauty, down another road there is a place that could use something beautiful.

And so it is with our lives. We daily come to intersections where decisions must be made that will spur us on to either love more deeply or search for love more frantically. This shocking truth remains: the people who indulge themselves in the Red Light District in Amsterdam desire to be loved as much as any professing Christian on planet Earth. In fact, if I am reading my Bible correctly, it's the women in the sex shops who find Jesus so attractive, and it's the people in the tamer parts of the city—in the evangelical churches, for instance—who find Jesus rather dull. The woman who broke the alabaster jar, for example, may know these streets well.

The attraction of the woman who stands in the window wearing only underwear, or at least some tiny pieces of fabric masquerading as underwear, to Jesus may just be because she understands that the Red Light District isn't just where she works, but it's also where she lives. On the days where she wanders out of the Red Light District into greener pastures, she suddenly begins to suffocate because she is so desperate for grace. In Jesus she finds that loving embrace, but on the chance that no one shows her the love of Christ, she will return to more comfortable surroundings—red lights that no longer mean stop, but simply remind her that she has gone too far.

While I have never lived in the actual Red Light District in Amsterdam, I do know that I have often gone too far away from

A Time to Question Everything

that which is good, right, and true to feel at home in the church. And there are times when I am convinced that, were my heart to be revealed, I would be completely rejected by all men and women everywhere. Dostoyevsky writes, "One can love one's neighbors in the abstract or even at a distance, but at close quarters it's almost impossible."[1] The kind of love our hearts long for isn't normal. It's a passionate grace that embraces us while we live in the Red Light District and doesn't wait for us to be different. Grace itself is a cleansing agent that is the only antidote for our conflicted hearts.

And our hearts are conflicted. We want everyone else to change before we do. We want the world to change before the church does. We want to be saved without giving up sin. We are conflicted. John Newton puts it this way:

> I would not indulge vain reasonings concerning the counsels, ways, and providences of God; yet I am prone to do it. That the judge of all the earth will do right, is to me as evident and necessary as that two and two make four. I believe that he has a sovereign right to do what he will with his own, and that this sovereignty is but another name for the unlimited exercise of wisdom and goodness. But, my reasonings are often such, as if I had never heard of these principles, or had formally renounced them. I feel the workings of a presumptuous spirit that would account for everything and venture to dispute whatever it cannot comprehend. What an evil this is for a potsherd of the earth to contend with its Maker![2]

Newton wrote the most-sung hymn in modern church history, "Amazing Grace," but he lived with the knowledge that he himself wasn't so amazing. Grace was indeed so precious to Newton precisely because of his own awareness of deep inner conflict. In Romans 7:15, we simply read these words: "I do not understand my own actions. For I do not do what I want, but I do the very thing I hate." This is why everyone needs grace.

Dostoyevsky continues,

---

1. Dostoyevsky, *Gospel in Dostoyevsky*, 44.
2. Newton, *Letters of John Newton*, 130.

Who Did You Notice Today?

> On earth, however, we are as it were astray, and if it were not for the precious image of Christ before us, we should be undone and altogether lost, like the human race before the flood. Much on earth is hidden from us, but to make up for that we have been given a mysterious hidden longing for our living bond with the other world.[3]

That other world is given to us by grace alone.

I am convinced that the primary reason people do not chase after the gospel or respond to the gospel message with humility is precisely because we long for grace but so often get rules instead. And the reason we so often get rules, is because grace is far too messy to enter into lightly. Authentic grace will scandalize the church and disrupt our own lives. The woman who is prostituting herself in the window who experiences grace can become your sister in Christ overnight. On one evening she could be standing nude in a shop window and then lying with three different men, only to later be on her knees before God. Within a few short hours she is sitting next to you in church. There are no rules to explain such a turnaround. Our brains don't comprehend the scene unless, of course, we understand that the shop window is also a mirror. To see through to the woman many call a prostitute, we must first look at ourselves. Suddenly, the Red Light District is home to us as well because we too run through the red lights daily in search of love and desperate for intimacy.

So, getting up from the fall isn't easy nor is it done quickly. Instead, it's a difficult journey where we carry crosses and become more aware of our need for grace. Why so difficult? Why anticipate getting a little dirty? Because if we're truly going to experience life-altering, Christ-exalting, scandalous grace, then this is going to get messy. Your clothes are going to get dirty, your hands will be filthy, and you'll eventually want to feel clean. You're going to want to use something other than the filthy rags we've been using to clean off. If we use our time well, then you and I will eventually give up trying to bathe ourselves and simply ask God for rain. When it pours, we will stand in the puddles, feel the mud squeeze between

---

3. Dostoyevsky, *Gospel in Dostoyevsky*, 249.

our toes, and for the first time in a long time we will feel clean again. Soaked through to the bone, we may shiver a bit, but it will be worth it. Experiencing authentic grace and the deep truth of the gospel is always worth a little mess.

Grace breaks through the mess and begins to make something beautiful out of something marred and broken. I heard a teacher once say that the lines on our respective faces are evidence of God's grace in our lives. In other words, as we endure a broken world and as we engage in a lifelong quest to push back the effects of the fall, we will most definitely cry tears of pain, lose sleep at night, and feel the world beat against our very soul. Following a man who has stripes on his back will mostly likely draw lines and deep circles under our eyes and on our faces at the very least. Dare we follow Jesus into painful places? Well, we have no choice if it's Jesus we're following. Part of following Jesus is to pay attention to your surroundings. So we travel away from Amsterdam and begin again a journey where we are all students (disciples) who are marked by curiosity and compassion. An insatiable appetite to learn more and experience more of the grace of Jesus, and an incurable compulsion to heal the brokenhearted are subjects for disciples to learn. We all could learn to care for the wounded, and walk with the poor as we learn love.

We started this journey in the Red Light District of Amsterdam, but we will continue on the streets of New Orleans. Six months after Hurricane Katrina flooded 80 percent of the city, I was walking the streets with friends from Urban Impact. This is a local nonprofit affiliated with the Evangelical Free Church and is dedicated to community development in the inner city of New Orleans. We drove past the broken levees and walked down parts of the lower ninth ward and other neighborhoods. There were no sex shops or half-naked women beckoning us to stop. There were no crowded pubs or lines of tourists snapping pictures. In fact, there were hardly any people at all. Instead of red lights, there were red numbers posted on the outside of the homes to instruct relief teams and emergency personnel of the number of dead bodies found inside. The vast majority of the houses we were driving

Who Did You Notice Today?

by had a number one or two, sometimes even a three, written on the front door.

On one street, we saw a church group from the Midwest helping to clean out a deserted house. Most of them were college-age kids or high school-age kids who would probably never have come to the poor, poverty-stricken neighborhood before Katrina hit. But now the streets were deserted and there were more tasks to be done than people to talk to. The storm had made everything look poor, so visiting work crews could quite possibly miss the fact that these neighborhoods were racked with neglect and a lack of love long before the winds and waves crashed against their shores. The red numbers for me came to mean far more than a body count after a terrible hurricane. They became symbolic of every neighborhood in the world and they remain a reminder that each house that we pass by has at least one body inside. And that body belongs to a human being, and that human being longs to be loved by another human being. The red numbers on the doors may as well have been the red letters in the New Testament because I felt that, in a very real way, Jesus was speaking to those who passed by, saying, 'love your neighbor as you love yourself.'

When Jesus was asked to summarize the law or to single out the most vital command to follow, he answered in two ways. He gave a command and then an illustration, just in case anyone missed the clarity of the command. The command was rather straightforward: "Love the Lord you God with all that you have and love your neighbor as yourself," (Luke 10:27). The illustration came after Jesus was pressed for details. A man asked him, "Who is my neighbor?" In other words, if I am supposed to love my neighbor, let me know who those people are, because surely I am not being asked to love everyone.

Jesus tells the story of the good Samaritan. This story is so shocking, so compelling, and so profoundly universal, that even our own government has a set of good Samaritan laws. For example, if you're the first car to arrive at the scene of an accident, by law, you must stop.[4] The story Jesus told was shocking because the

---

4. See also http://www.ilga.gov/legislation/ilcs/ilcs3.asp?ActID=2076&

A Time to Question Everything

hero was an outcast and someone that the Jewish church leaders despised. The story is compelling because a man is lying next to the road, dying after thieves steal his things and beat him senseless. The story is universal because at some point in our lives, we will all be on the side of some road literally or figuratively, hoping someone will stop to help us out. On the Gulf Coast, the entire region was left beaten and half dead, waiting for someone to come and help. But people kept walking by and the help was slow in arriving. Huddled together in the Superdome, residents of New Orleans wondered if anyone cared. Who will pick them up, take them to safety, bandage their wounds, and meet their needs? Now there were dozens and dozens of good Samaritans and heroic acts of mercy in the wake of Katrina, but for me, the hurricane has come to be symbolic. It's one of those natural tests or a pop quiz for the North Americans who attend church. The whole country knows that the Gulf Coast is in need, now who is going to love that region back to health?

Katrina didn't just impose her will on a helpless shoreline, she also exposed us in so many ways. My own emotions ran the gamut. I was in awe of the power of nature, but I was angry at the disorganization of the government. I was amazed at the amount of money given but disgusted at the selfishness that prevented (and still does prevent) the cash from getting directly to the needy in a timely fashion.

Dealing with Ourselves First

Yet Larry Crabb is right when he says, "Revival in the church must begin with revolution in the soul. It does no good, and actually does great harm, to fuss about church until first we fuss about ourselves."[5] And I have had my fill of editorials that have criticized people in the wake of Katrina. I never once heard a politician "fuss" about themselves, nor did I hear celebrities "fuss" about

---

ChapterID=58.

5. Crabb, *Pressure's Off*, 50.

themselves. The harsh reality, though, is that I didn't fuss much about myself either until I was standing outside of a house with a red number one on the door. A single body lying dead inside and for days no one stopped by to help.

God used Katrina to preach a sermon and she bellowed out in her category four and five voice "Do you love your neighbor?" So even before leaving New Orleans I started to fuss about myself. Do I love those who may not love me back? Do I love people well? Do I stop to help those in need or am I just too busy? Do I see the bodies inside the houses I pass as real people who have real needs?

A story from upstate New York, published in February of 2007, stays with me. An elderly man, whose wife had died a few years earlier, was found dead in his house. When he was found, he had been dead for over a year! He was slumped in front of the television and no one thought to look for him, stop by to say hello, or even wonder where he went. He would not have been found were it not for a harsh winter storm and water pipes bursting in the house. I wonder if there were people who call themselves Christian, who lived on his street and, when asked about the Christian faith, would reply, "oh, it's summarized in the command to love one's neighbor." Our faith is no good at all if not expressed in love.

The people of New Orleans didn't cry out with new laws for us to follow, but they simply pointed out that our laws mean nothing if they are not soaked in love. On the streets of the lower ninth ward, people were not wondering if I was an adulterer, a liar, a thief, or even a murderer. I was just being asked, at the heart level, a rather pointed question: Do you love people? If you do, the Bible tells us that love covers a multitude of sins. In 1 Corinthians 13:13, we read that there is "faith, hope, and love. But the greatest of these is love." Why? When faith will lead to salvation and hope will get you through the trials of life, why is love the greatest? I believe it's because God loves. God doesn't need hope or faith, so love is the one out of the three with the most direct link to divinity. God doesn't need hope, He knows everything. And God doesn't live by faith, because He is self-sufficient and all-powerful. But God shows love, exercises love, showers us with love, sends his only Son out of love, and chases down prodigals out of love. And if we love people, we do what God would do.

So, I am fussing about myself and I am struggling with the reality that I often trust people and I often hope that people will come through for me, but I fall dramatically short when it comes to loving people. There are plenty of storms assaulting neighborhoods around our country, so what am I waiting for? Before Katrina hit, there were warnings to evacuate. These warnings were not met with immediate action, instead there were significant delays and a rather poor emergency plan. The buses were not ready, the police were not given reserve ammunition or back-up soldiers, and the communication lines were not clear. While those are realities, that's not fussing about myself. For the record, by fussing, I mean that space between reflection and conviction where you know you need to make some changes. Some events mark us that way.

For me, I must grapple with the fact that I drive by homes where marriages are breaking apart, children struggle with depression, young girls have eating disorders, and young boys spend little or no time with their father. And these houses are not in poor, neglected neighborhoods. These are well-kept homes in well-maintained subdivisions. I suppose I am slow to respond because the meltdown of the family is not even considered by many to be a category four or five hurricane; we have downgraded divorce and depression to tropical storms. And there is hardly any attention paid in the news to a tropical storm. Single families in need typically get neglected until the entire neighborhood suffers. Just ask any single mother in any large city in this country who loves them the most. But, we must understand, that single families are the spinal cords of neighborhoods and if the families disintegrate, so goes the neighborhood.

I know who my neighbors are and my guess is that you do too. We just don't like the reality that God's neighborhood is so much larger than we had expected. If you're like me, you thought you were just joining a church when God was actually signing us up for a spiritual war complete with dead bodies, injured family members, and half-naked men and women strewn about the ground waiting for help. "Christians are as burnt out as pagans, sometimes more. We're discouraged with ourselves and how life is turning out for us. We thought for years it would be different."[6] We sincerely thought that the crosses we would bear would be gold or silver and they would hang symbolically around our necks. Instead, we find out as we grow closer to Christ that the cross is real, the blood spilled on the ground is real, the tears we cry are real, and when we hurt, when we stumble uphill, Jesus tells us to still love our neighbor. Despite the messiness of our own hearts and the messed up situation of our neighbor, Jesus says to lay your life down for them and to love them well. If you love people, you will silence the potential critics. If you hand out cups of cold water, you will summarize the law of God. If you visit the widows, take in the orphans, and don't forget those who are in prison, you will show that the Bible isn't an antiquated book, but a living reality that pierces the heart.

Yet somehow, people who struggle, people who understand their own need for redemption, draw near to Jesus. Why is it that a man who sets an example that is far more difficult to follow than anyone else on planet Earth continues to be so alluring and so attractive?

So if loving Jesus were quite easy, so would loving people. Life isn't easy, loving people isn't easy, and we underestimate the difficulty of love way too much. The command, you must recall, is to love God, not just believe in God. Faith is necessary, but the greatest of these is love.

And only love that is laced with supernatural wonder can endure the pain of the world we currently live in. So, when we say we follow Jesus, we do so as men and women prepared not only to sacrifice comfort and convenience, but as men and women who are prepared to stop and listen to the cries of those who have been left on the side of the road or who are writhing in emotional pain inside a lonely house somewhere.

Can you hear your neighbor's cry for help? Let me put it differently. When you were down and out, do you remember who

6. Ibid., 150.

heard you cry out and do you remember who stopped and lifted you out of the hole you were in? Did that person have lines on their face and, if so, aren't you grateful for the storms God has brought them through prior to their meeting you in your time of need?

We don't yet live in a world that is overflowing with good Samaritans. Traveling through the Red Light District of Amsterdam, I was reminded not only of my own shortcomings, but of the incredible grace and steadfast love of a man named Jesus, who not only was known as a lover of people, but also a friend of sinners. Walking through storm-ravaged New Orleans, I was reminded of my own neglect of not only the poor, but of entire neighborhoods, and I have to look in the mirror and wrestle with whether or not I am willing to follow wherever Jesus leads.

Is grace big enough to change me from the inside out?

6

Why Am I Afraid to Sleep?

"I've always envied people who sleep easily. Their brains must be cleaner, the floorboards of the skull well swept, all the little monsters closed up in a steamer trunk at the foot of the bed."

—David Benioff, *City of Thieves*

SEVERAL YEARS AGO, I was standing in the midst of a backyard celebration following a wedding rehearsal. The ideas of love, adulthood, and lifelong commitment filled my mind as I thought through the reason for our gathering. I was delivering the message the next day at the wedding.

While scores of friends and family drank beer, wine, and other celebratory drinks, I held on to my sixteen-ounce bottle of Mountain Dew.

"I thought you would have outgrown that stuff by now," said the bride's father.

"But I like the taste," I replied.

"How old are you?" he said.

A Time to Question Everything

I said nothing. I didn't know what to say. I don't know if it was the tone of his voice or simply the fact that I had no witty reply. But there I stood in my late twenties about to deliver a sermon on someone's big day, still drinking the same Mountain Dew I downed when I was thirteen and complaining about math homework. I was wallowing in my own insecurity and my knees were shaking so violently I had to sit. My right leg began bobbing up and down, when the question finally came.

"So, how's a lifestyle marked by anxiety working for you?" said Dr. Phil, or at least that's what was going on in my mind.

I said nothing. My leg continued to move, but more like a piston trying to start an engine than like a nervous twitch. I wanted to spew out a few words of profanity, but I had to give a sermon in less than twenty-four hours on the biggest day of someone else's life. For a few seconds, I regretted my ordination vows and thought about the freedom of speech enjoyed by so many others outside of public ministry. Then I reminded myself that this was all over a bottle of green soda, laced with as much sugar as the FDA will allow and the caffeine intake of at least three cups of coffee. Surely I am the most seriously messed up person in the world.

In fact, later on I was glad about drinking the Mountain Dew as I reviewed my sermon late in to the evening hours. Preachers can screw up in a lot of services, but weddings are not one of them. Families, as a general rule, are so much more merciful at a funeral than a wedding. As my notes became second nature, I readied myself for bed, but to the chagrin of myself and surely the delight of the bride's father if he knew, I could not sleep. Luckily, I had a bottle of prescription sleeping pills nearby. Ninety minutes and one little pill later, I was resting peacefully until morning.

When the sun shone again, the effect of the medication remained. So I got up in search of a strong cup of coffee. In fact, during morning prayers, I even thanked God that there was a Starbucks on every other city block, inside bookshops, and even in grocery stores. I was so happy about this reality that I didn't even question the stupidity of paying four dollars for a cup of coffee. In fact, I filled my travel mug full so that my legal drug addiction

Why Am I Afraid to Sleep?

could come with me to the church for final preparations. I have never, until now, even questioned the need for coffee before speaking publicly at a wedding as if my central nervous system needed the reminder to wake up. Rather, I freely admit that without Starbucks, the lasting effect of sleeping pills would plague me like the hangover I could've had if I wasn't so stuck on drinking the Mountain Dew instead of the beer or wine.

I am pleased to report that the couple was happily married, the bride's father walked steadily down the aisle, and that I am now in my mid-forties and drinking a healthy mix of red wine, the contemplative Scotch, and yes, the occasional Mountain Dew.

To this day, I can't remember which came first, my caffeine addiction or my insomnia. And frankly, I don't care, because I remember the Sabbath and look forward to learning what that word means in the coming days.

In Search of Rest

In 1989, I began college in Pella, Iowa, at the creatively named Central College. Scores of sleepless nights were spent trying to get a higher letter grade by cramming literally hundreds of books into my brain. Other sleepless nights were spent trying to fall in and out of love, solidify friendships, prank other dormitory residents, and eat pancakes at Happy Chef. During exam weeks, I would get up on Monday morning and begin cramming, not sleeping once until the tests were complete. Sometimes that would be two days, sometimes less. Maybe these exam weeks ruined my sleep habits, but I had started drinking caffeinated beverages so much earlier in life. Does caffeine feed insomnia or vice versa?

Shrugging off the need to lower my caffeine intake, I begin to blame insomnia on other more substantive and spiritual things. Maybe my restlessness increased when I stayed up late listening to the sobs of a young woman whose boyfriend had pressured her in to having an abortion. Then there's the drunken man who wondered how his DUI would impact his future and the woman who described the horrible night when she was brutally raped. These all seem like good reasons to lie awake at night.

On a more personal level, maybe I began tossing and turning when I realized that my conduct didn't match my convictions. Hypocrisy and guilt plagued me at times (and still does) when I thought of unkind words said, unwillingness to lend a helping hand, compulsion for more than a goodnight kiss, and desire to pursue career rather than Christ.

Perhaps that's the most amazing thing to me about Jesus. He never lay awake at night struggling with the guilt of personal sin. Instead, he stayed awake one night praying over the effects of my sin. Jesus knows that I am a seriously messed up person and yet he died, rose again, and continues to pray for me anyway. Despite the utter pollution of my own soul, I am loved without condemnation, reservation, or hesitation.

More disturbing though, is that the world may just be filled with people like me. Whether you call people sinners or not, I am not the only one who drinks Mountain Dew past the age of thirty, nor am I the only fan of Starbucks. My doctor assures me that other people take medication to help them sleep and a psychiatrist I visited for a while says that it's almost normal. By the way, I didn't understand a lot of what the psychiatrist said, so I quit going, which is also normal, I am told.

During two summers in college, I worked as a camp counselor at a rather unusual camp. Every single child had a disability of some sort. Children ranging in age from grade school to eighteen years old came to have a good time. A few of them were strategically placed to help me grow up. One day in particular at that camp haunts me. A boy with learning disabilities and a physical disability that caused him to walk with an odd gait that sometimes looked like a limp, ran away from his parents when they arrived to pick him up. Camp week ended and he had been fine all week. In fact, he had been more than fine, he swam, went fishing, and by all external signals, enjoyed himself.

When I finally found him, he was sobbing in the corner of one of the dorm rooms.

Why Am I Afraid to Sleep?

"I hate you," he said.

"What do you mean?" I replied.

"You made me have fun this week and now I have to go home," he said.

I had no reply. I sat down and hugged him. He cried a bit more on my shoulder before we walked out to the driveway together. What I didn't say earlier is that this boy walked with a limp because of physical and emotional abuse. He was continually shuffled around in search of a home. The very thing that he looked forward to each summer made the wounds worse; the joy reminded him of the pain. A week with fishing, swimming, boat rides, and new friends seemed to be a budding rosebush in a desert. The last day of camp simply reminded him that the rest of life wasn't fun and games. Tossing and turning over people like that makes sense to me.

So, the disciples were right to ask Jesus, "Don't you care?" when they found him sleeping during a violent storm on the open sea (Mark 4:35). These were fishermen, after all, and wouldn't scare easily. People who made their livelihoods on the sea could tell when bad weather would be threatening or merely theatrical and these men felt threatened while Jesus lay sleeping. No wonder some people think God is snoozing as the world spins out of control. After all, there are so many of us who cannot sleep, we wonder how can an eternally loving God find any rest at all? The storms of life threaten to kill us and there's Jesus, hitting the snooze button.

Peace. Be still.

When Jesus finally gets out of bed, that's what he says and that's what we all want to hear. The wind and the waves obeyed immediately, while most of humanity frantically runs around, afraid that the storms of life are just too much. The reason may just lie in the fact that we don't really know how to rest. I don't know how to rest. The more poignant question though is: Do I want to find rest?

The answer on most days is a resounding "I think so." In a world filled with cell phones, pagers, the internet, instant banking, and express lines, I think I want to find rest. And I am pretty sure I want peace. I just don't know if I am ready to sacrifice keeping up with what has been labeled cultural progress. Let's be brutally honest. We don't rest more easily at night because our teenage sons and daughters have cell phones. If we do, what does that say about parents twenty years ago? What does it say about our own faith? If God is in control, it's stressful, but if my child has a cell phone, that's peace of mind? So we hand out the cell phone and still pace back and forth at night waiting for them to come home. As the hours grow late, we put on a pot of coffee so as to be alert, just in case. And when our child arrives home and is safely tucked in bed, we lie wide awake in our own beds confessing to be Christian and saying prayers like "thank God, she's home" or "whew, thank the Lord he didn't do anything stupid."

Having a teenager with a cell phone doesn't bring peace of mind, it simply brings another phone bill. Do we really not worry about a sixteen-year-old girl driving home late at night, alone, because she has a smart phone with the latest apps? We worry because of those other people driving as well. The truck drivers who carry a thermos full of caffeine because they must get their shipment to the destination on time are also on the road. The salesmen who have spent the vast majority of the week traveling are driving too. Let's not forget other teenagers, daydreamers, and the graveyard shift of factory workers.

In other words, traveling the roads together are a bunch of sleep-deprived, caffeine-addicted people who think the other driver is the problem. Of course, none of this enters my mind as I get into my own car and drive around listening to instrumental music, trying to relax, so that I can go home and sleep. I am trying to drive my way out of anxiety. Unfortunately, I am also hungry, so I drive by the local Taco Bell, which is conveniently open until two in the morning for seriously messed up people like me. I order a grilled chicken soft taco because it sounds healthier than a bean burrito after midnight. The soda is mandatory to wash down the flour tortilla. And off I go, with a taco, a soda, and modern chill music to cap off a rather stressful day. Surely, this will help me wind down and get the rest I so desperately need.

Why Am I Afraid to Sleep?

When I finally get home, I run straight to the medicine cabinet and take a Zantac. This will reduce the acid in my stomach which is necessary now, after the late-night taco and soda. Finally, my head hits the pillow just five hours before my breakfast meeting with a couple whose high school student hates church. I am not looking forward to the meeting at all. This student has not lifted a finger to serve the church, hates the popular kids, and shows up once a month for youth meetings. Besides, the coffee at the restaurant, while cheaper than Starbucks, tastes like Columbian Kool-Aid. Every time I eat there, I look for the dog dish under the table in which to pour out this sad excuse for a drink. But then again, I haven't slept well and could use the caffeine. Bad coffee is better than no coffee at all.

"Our child just hates going to church," begins one of the concerned parents. I sit as patiently as I can and listen to forty reasons why worship is boring, high school students are critical, and some children, even Christian teenagers, are mean-spirited. By the time one of the parents comes up for air from their dive into an ocean of complaints, a half an hour has slipped away.

"How can I help you?" I reply.

Suddenly, the other parent, on cue, chimes in and takes their half an hour to explain to me the sins of this generation and their concern for the future. I am glad that the caffeine hasn't fully kicked in and my mind wanders off at times. I am especially happy that my thoughts are not yet publicized. All that is running through my mind are phrases, not complete sentences; questions without any good answers.

For example, if these parents are so concerned about the faith and moral conduct of teenagers, why do they model such incessant discontent with their own religion? And is the fact that high school students are often critical of one another really a new idea? My favorite of their concerns, though, remains the idea that worship services are boring. Students, of course, habitually neglect worship every other day of the week, so Sunday morning is challenging simply by being different. The command to keep the Sabbath competes with the demands of everyday life.

A Time to Question Everything

Then, there's the activity of Saturday night. Are we really asking students to be fully engaged and alert at nine in the morning the day after they have typically stayed out late with friends doing God knows what? Unfortunately, most students who deprive themselves of rest on Saturday night also forego caffeine on Sunday morning. And there they sit, sandwiched in between mom and dad, nodding off during an explanation of John's Gospel, jolted awake on the closing, triumphant hymn.

"So, what are we going to do?" asks the couple across from me.

I stare at them with no immediate response. Everything running through my head cannot be said in public without negative consequences. They want their student to have fun, crave attendance, and be really nice to people. In other words, the student desires church without desiring God. Even the most secular people in the world understand that without a changed heart, church attendance is virtually meaningless. Sitting in worship daydreaming about being elsewhere is the epitome of pointlessness.

"Let's continue to meet and help each other out," I reply.

"But what are we going to do?" ask the couple again.

"Honestly, I don't know," I reply.

The couple is totally frustrated. Seeking God for answers to life's problems seems lazy to them. Surely prayer isn't nearly as effective as a brand-new program. One last plea from the couple, exasperated with me now, to intervene with a new Saturday night activity, a canoe trip, or some fun way to get their child to fall in love with church. I have no such answer. I am concerned that the programs offered up to young people in church have become less discipleship and more distraction.

The rest of the day, I want to quit ministry of any kind. I can't really articulate my reasons, I just want to quit. The whole charade on Sunday morning seems overwhelming. One generation tells another generation that organ music is holy, having fun is a civic and sacred right, and prayer is a last resort. In my own heart, the love that is uncritical and unconditional is running away and being replaced by a cynicism that is fed regularly by my own insomnia.

Why Am I Afraid to Sleep?

And my own world seems at times on the verge of falling apart. After all, the entire world falls apart on a few hours' sleep.

I am fed up with the idea of polite Christianity and want to tear down crosses everywhere. People who wear a cross, the sign of great suffering in the life of Jesus the Christ for all of humanity, can, on occasion, drive me insane. These same people will avoid pain with maximum strength medication, complain about the speed of their microwave, and lament the long commute to work from the suburbs where the houses have multi-car garages. It's a joke that isn't funny. I am not laughing. Instead, I am frightened that I may be more like the cross-wearing complainers than the Christ who bore the cross.

Instead of someone standing for truth, I feel like I have sold out to a culture that doesn't hold life as sacred, thinks liberty is personal, not communal, and that the pursuit of happiness eclipses all other virtues. The spiritual cost for selling out has been incredibly subtle and unbelievably high. What do I mean? Church attendance doesn't change the world, love does. Being nice doesn't mean I am Christian. If we don't have anything worth dying for, are we really living a productive life? I turn to God often with questions and even demand answers at times in my immature prayers. Why don't people repent and change more often? How can we live with so much information and so little sacrificial kindness? These thoughts linger in my mind as I stare out into the abyss, lying awake again on my bed. My wife is asleep next to me with one leg outside and one leg inside the blankets. This one leg in and one leg out posture is really a thermostat regulating her own body heat throughout the night. It's kind of funny and really cute.

I have tried to explain to her my struggles, but I fumble poorly through those conversations. What comes out is a garbled mess of emotional rubbish that is barely cohesive. I barely live with myself; I don't understand why anyone else does. I sometimes think that my wife is the "for better" and I am the "for worse" part of the deal. Sometimes, I am afraid to ask her what she thinks about me.

A Time to Question Everything

Know My Anxious Thoughts

I fear either personal insanity, or at minimum a nagging anxiety that some things may never change. What happens if the preachers simply impart knowledge, but live like everyone else? What happens if the church spends most of its budget on its own building, while the poor and marginalized are broken down and in need of help? How can the church gripe and complain about homosexual unions when so many of the heterosexual marriages end in divorce? What happens if things don't change for the better?

Edward Welch writes that "Worriers are visionaries minus the optimism. An experienced worrier can go for days from past to future and back again, never landing in the present."[1] While it's strangely encouraging to be labeled a visionary, I must confess that Welch is more correct than is comfortable to admit. I have no idea how many days I have let slip by because I have either overanalyzed the past or have been paralyzed about the future.

We brought our daughter home for the first time during a November snowstorm in St. Louis. My wife was justifiably wiped out from the delivery and we had our daughter bundled up as best we could. Our son, who was born twenty months earlier, was waiting at home with his maternal grandparents. The problem was this: our son was not feeling well. In fact, he was not feeling well at all. So, in the middle of an early snowstorm, I drove my wife and daughter home. I walked them inside the house and then picked up my son and immediately drove to the doctor's office as he had developed a fever that had increased. We had a three-day-old daughter and a sick twenty-month-old boy. Our son eventually fought off a viral infection of some kind after we kept him quarantined from his sister for several days. This was day one of a fresh sense of helplessness and anxiety.

Three years later, my wife phoned me and told me to meet her at the Urgent Care facility. Our son had broken his arm in a freak accident at preschool. When I arrived, my son had already been crying and was obviously favoring his left arm. The doctor

---

1. Welch, *Running Scared*, 50.

came out and said: "Ok, which one of you wants to help me with the x-ray?"

I stood up, with my son in my arms, and followed the doctor in another room. My son was scared and truth be told, so was I. He was in great pain and I couldn't do a blasted thing about it. In fact, I was about to make it worse.

Because my son had broken his arm in a rather odd spot, right near his elbow, we needed to straighten his arm a bit to get a clear X-ray. My job was to hold my son's arm against a flat surface so that the picture and, subsequently, the diagnosis would come out clearly. Yet, every time I tried to straighten my son's broken arm, my only boy screamed, tears streaming down his face, his little body writhing in pain. Unable to get a quality pose and thus a clear picture, the doctor was growing impatient. Finally, the doctor came toward me and said:

"Do you want me to hold him down?"

I responded with as stern a voice as I have ever used to a complete stranger and with a tone of voice that made the doctor stop and simply look at me.

"No. You do not need to hold my son. I will hold my son," I said. Tears welling up in my own eyes, I simply stared at the doctor until he nodded. We eventually got the x-ray. I never once let go of my son.

As I write this, tears still come to my eyes, not only because I can still hear my only son scream, "Daddy, no...it hurts, Daddy..." but also because deep down, I know I am not enough to push back the effects of the fall. Sometimes I can't make things better or make the pain go away or keep people from crying. Sometimes, all I know how to do is hold on, trusting that what is broken will one day be made right again.

7

How Can We Voice Frustration?

> "The urge to shout filthy words at the top of his voice was as strong as ever."
>
> —George Orwell, *1984*

THERE'S A LOT GOING on in this world to cuss about. And I don't think that words like "shucks" and "gee whiz" capture what we're trying to say when we express anger over injustice, war, poverty, and well, anything more significant than our favorite team losing or when we cannot find the remote control to the television.

Profanity can be vulgar and offensive. Profanity can also make a statement when frustration boils over. Take for example, the devoted father who invites his eldest son to help with a house project. The hammer misses the nail, but nails the thumb and suddenly, in a flurry of adrenaline and anger, the little bonding moment is ruined. Then, there is the mother in the kitchen who is a flurry of activity in preparation for the guests to arrive. In haste, one of the trophy glasses, the ones that sit in the dining room where no one ever eats, in an expensive cabinet made solely for things no one ever uses, crashes to the ground. While the

How Can We Voice Frustration?

rest of the known universe stops in breathless anticipation, mom screams out obscenities and vulgarities that would get any grade school kid suspended, any high school kid a detention, and any well-meaning employee fired. Four letter words fly everywhere and those watching actually duck, physically trying to thwart the onslaught of words. Yet, because this glass was handmade and a family heirloom, blown by her grandfather in his own garage, the week after her grandmother died, some new words made their way into the family scrapbook. These words remain far more colorful than any of the standard four-letter ones and, to this day, I won't repeat them.

In the recent economic turmoil amidst a tanking economy, I can imagine the white-collar Wall Street brokers sitting around saying all kinds of things we should never say. I can't imagine them saying, "Wow, that's not very swell at all." Nor can I, though I have tried, imagine their families saying, "Gee, that doesn't sound like much fun." Instead, I presume these rather hardworking men and women resorted to profanity not to describe the moment, but to cope with the situation. Therein lies the beauty, if there is such a thing, of profanity. The point is made quickly, briefly, and rather strikingly.

Let's be honest with one another. After you hear your mother say, "Why can't anyone build a vacuum cleaner that works better than this piece of horsesh#?" the world is forever changed. Innocence is lost and is difficult to regain. It's as if the black-and-white television suddenly changed into a colorful home theatre system with surround sound. Nothing is the same. This woman who tucks you in at night, who reads you bedtime stories, who makes breakfast with slippers on, is now the woman who can blurt out descriptions of animal excrement at any moment. These amazing little words called "profanity" have changed everything.

Anatomical aids aside, many socially conscious conservatives have been trying to avoid the use of such foul language for many decades. Ironically, these same people get into the same situations as any of the men and women who cuss like sailors but, instead of resorting to the evil words, they use substitutes. And they end up producing a sanitized and acceptable version that simply changes the outside, while neglecting the inside. And the result looks and sounds ridiculous. We can applaud the restraint, but it feels less than authentic.

I don't know the name of the first person that used "heck" instead of "hell." And I don't know whose bright idea it was to say "shucks," "gee whiz," or "darn." I suppose these people remain proud of themselves for being, well, nice, or maybe they were being polite and just plain kind. And to some small degree, we should thank these people. But that's it, nothing more than a simple, plain, black-and-white, thank-you card. And we will sign the card, "Sincerely yours," neatly blocked and left justified.

I picture them greeting one another on the street and exchanging pleasantries dripping with syrup.

"How are you today?" one asks.

"Very well, thank you," the other replies.

"Glad it stopped raining," the first continues.

"Yeah, it should be a very nice day," the other says.

Suddenly, a car rushes by through a giant puddle of water, soaking the two people on the sidewalk. Water jumps from the street and now drips from their faces. One man's hat has been knocked to the ground and lies dirty and exhausted from the beating.

"Aw, shucks," says one man.

"Golly. That darn driver seems to have done that on purpose," says the other man.

Bending down to pick up his hat, one notices that there is a little clump of mud already beginning to soak into the inside bill. The hat is lifeless and slumped over. The man's face sinks into disappointment and then to anger before settling on frustration.

"What the heck was that driver doing?" he asks.

"I know what you mean. Gee whiz, you would think he'd be a little nicer," says the other.

A week later, these same two men find themselves on the identical corner. One man is carrying a sack of groceries and the

How Can We Voice Frustration?

other is simply strolling along. In a moment of déjà vu, they remember everything out loud.

"Last week, we were standing in this very spot, do you remember?" one says.

"Yeah, and then that one driver rushed through the puddle, spraying mud and water all over us," says the other.

They smile and put their arms around each other, resembling old war buddies more than saccharine-sweet nobodies. As they start across the street, walking on the right side of the crosswalk, a skateboarder zooms by, bumping into the one man and causing his sack of groceries to fall all over the street. Before the man can utter a sound, the skateboarder vanishes. These two etiquette veterans promptly drop to their knees and scoop up the stray food in record time. Once on the other side of the street, the one man reorganizes the now-ransacked bag of groceries.

"Darn these insensitive young people," he says.

"Golly, that skateboarder didn't even seem to care. What the heck is this world coming to?" says the other man.

"I know what you mean. One minute you are minding your own business, when all of a sudden this blasted, disrespectful bloke knocks into you," one man says.

"Shucks, you're right," says the other man.

"One of these days you'll be sorry," yells the one man to the vanished skateboarder.

The other man flashes a victory smile and they part company, once again triumphant. Some people would have screamed and shouted all kinds of things, but not the kind, courteous, and nice people who have brought us such wonderful little phrases like "you're swell," and "gadzooks." Oh, these people shouted all right, and in a rather angry tone of voice, but they shouted, "Hey there, do you want me to be rude to you?"

The next week passes in rather uneventful fashion as the two men arrive on the corner at different moments. They each briefly recall the previous two weeks, but quickly move on to urgent appointments. On the last week of the month, these legends of restraint find themselves once again face-to-face.

A Time to Question Everything

"Cross your fingers," says the one man. He has previously held a bag of groceries, but today he travels free of distraction.

"No kidding," says the other man.

The two walk briskly alongside the right portion of the crosswalk. Suddenly, without warning or notice, a pigeon dropping lands on the shoulder of the one man, sliding an inch down his jacket before coming to a complete stop. Upon reaching the other side of the street, the two men pause to assess the damage.

"Can you believe it? A bird went number two on my shoulder," says the fly-by victim.

"Holy cow, man, that just isn't right," says the other man.

"This corner has not been very nice to me," says the one man.

"You can say that again," says the other man.

The bird dropping stains the man's coat and upon reaching his house that day, greeting his wife with the usual pleasantry, he starts to recount the previous month on that dreaded corner. His wife listens intently to the car rushing by, the water splashing all over her husband, and the mud clinging to his hat. She listens quietly to the rude skateboarder who never even stopped to apologize after the groceries went all over the street. And today, a bird flew over and went number two on his shoulder, staining his coat, and dampening his otherwise good day.

"I feel cursed by that corner," he says.

His wife just smiles and says nothing.

"I mean it, I don't think I should travel that way for a while," he says.

His wife just sits, grinning from ear to ear.

"What? What is it? What's so funny?" he asks.

"Oh, it's nothing," she says.

"Come on, you're laughing at something," he says.

"It's nothing, I just think it's funny," she says.

"What's funny?"

"I can't believe a bird took a crap on your new coat. Honey, that really is miserable, but that's really funny," she says.

How Can We Voice Frustration?

He just sits there and says nothing while his beloved bride laughs uncontrollably. Sometimes, the words we are looking for are nowhere to be found. Darn.

Profanity in Our Culture

A dramatic pause seems to happen after an unexpected use of profanity. Filmmakers know this unwritten truth, which is why we should pause before purchasing our cinema tickets to understand what is really happening.

Words have the power to say who can see what film. After all, there is a certain level of language that allows only adults within the movie theatre, while a completely different set of words allows every conceivable age group. Walt Disney's dictionary is decidedly different than Martin Scorsese's. The thesaurus consulted by makers of *The Lion King* remains distinctively different than the one used by the makers of *Goodfellas*. This makes perfect sense to us.

And so there are little letters assigned to these little words. If a film is rated PG then you may hear a "damn," the misuse of the Lord's name, and well, the occasional bathroom allusion, but that's about it. And these words are used sparingly and for character effect. After all, adults paying attention to their role of parental guidance will certainly discourage such word usage around their own homes, but they may indeed slip up occasionally themselves. And that's exactly how they view such films.

"Oh, Billy, that man doesn't usually use those words, sometimes he just slips up, on a bad day, you know?" says one father to his son.

We call that conversation: PG.

These conversations, though, are not the ones that kids are trying to sneak into with fake identification cards. Students under the age of seventeen don't really care about the occasional slip; they care about the rants of sailors, the devil's tongue, and the kind of conversation that gets soap scrubbed into one's mouth. The film industry and subsequently the adult world assign a letter R to such words. The letter actually means "restricted," but no one really

A Time to Question Everything

pays attention to such a long word. The fourteen-year-old, after all, never understood that word.

"No running in the halls at school," says the teacher.

"But why?" whines the student body.

"Because that is a restricted action according to the student handbook," replies the school administrator.

Nonsense. That entire phrase makes absolutely no sense to the student body. And they actually look stupid immediately after the sentence is uttered and, as if looking for comfort, they turn to one another with quizzical looks wanting some support from one another that what they really did hear was a language they understood. So, well-meaning adults have devised an unintelligible scheme to discourage young people from viewing certain movies. And this scheme retains the unfortunate title of "restricted."

You know, Adam and Eve were actually in the first R-rated film when God told them that that tree over there, and especially the fruit attached to that tree, was restricted. You may eat from any other tree of the garden, but the tree in the middle of the garden, well, that's off limits. It's as if the entire garden was PG, except for the R-rated tree in the middle. The devil then comes along and says, "Restricted? What does that mean?"

Nothing has really changed since that fateful day when the woman gave to the husband and they both ate, suddenly seeing their nakedness. The only thing that has changed is how much of that nakedness could be seen by other people and what words can be heard by people in ear shot of the newly naked people.

The f-word, then, has become the R-word. Most people can deal with a lot of different uses of various other words, but for some reason, the f-word is intolerable in unrestricted areas. Restricted areas, are, after all, clearly marked with a big, capital letter. Any teenage boy or girl under the age of seventeen clearly sees the warning sign and understands the difference between restricted and unrestricted language.

The two previous conversations, rated PG and R respectively, remain quite obvious to the general public. There is the occasional slip and then there is the f-word, but along comes a newcomer

How Can We Voice Frustration?

to the rating neighborhood. The newcomer lives in an odd house that isn't offensive, but it isn't vogue either. People in the neighborhood, in fact, don't know what to do with such a place. And the newcomer is so temperamental that parents simply are confused as to whether or not their children will even play with that new family in the neighborhood.

One minute the new family will act like something out of the *Anne of Green Gables* series, while the next minute, they will act out some partially nude scene from *Sex and the City*. But most days are in between little Anne and a one-night stand, so the neighbors just throw up their hands in disbelief. The new family, in fact, becomes consistent dinner conversation around the cul-de-sac.

"I saw the new neighbor planting flowers in their garden," says one mother to her husband. The two kids listen to the horticultural observations of their parents, and these well-meaning parents let their children sit there in plain earshot of every word.

"Yeah, I saw that their perennials were coming up the other day," adds the surprisingly observant father.

Up to this point, the children seem rather bored, but at least are participants. These loving children are not left out of these tidbits of neighborhood news, but rather are brought fully into the conversation. Then, without warning, the father adds another observation.

"You know, after she finished gardening, our new neighbor, the wife anyway, sunbathed topless on the front lawn," says the father.

"She did what?" says the mother.

"She laid out on the blanket with her breasts in full view. I could see them quite clearly. I was rather surprised, but thought she knew what she was doing."

"Why would she lie nude in the front lawn? Is that allowed in this neighborhood? Can we just take our clothing off for everyone to see?" asks the mother.

Suddenly, the children's boredom vanishes, but so does the jovial nature of the parents. And so the conversation takes a rather awkward turn. For a few seconds, the flowers were beautiful,

65

admirable, and even enviable. Then, without warning, that same master gardener was lying out in the grass without a stitch of clothing covering her breasts. The conversation isn't boring at all, everyone is suddenly interested and paying attention, but the tension and awkwardness seems to leave a rather odd cloud hanging over the dinner table.

The label for such a conversation is PG-13, and it's this amazing little system of letters that educates parental figures today as to who should be allowed to see certain films. The language, of course, matches each letter. Parental guidance, after all, is never demanded, rather it's simply suggested. And suggesting parental guidance should give everyone a clue. After all, some movies are restricted for those under the age of 17 and other movies are suitable for those who are at least 13, but who are going with their parents. Thirteen-year-olds sitting with their parents, let's be honest, is one seriously confusing demographic. The Motion Picture Association of America deems this particular people group worthy of their own category.

We may feel that such ratings are inadequate then, but do we really have better ideas? Certainly a G-8 is out of the question, though rather tempting. Kids should be eight years old before seeing animated figures kiss each other. Then, there is the possible R-16. This makes a bigger deal of one's sixteenth birthday and also allows the f-word some breathing room. Senior citizens have no rating of their own, and so are relegated to the sophisticated-sounding term "classics."

Now, lest there be some kind of gross misunderstanding, I am not against rating movies at all. On the contrary, I am quite used to them and find them part of my daily routine. I actually count on them in much the same way that I count on the construction crews to delay traffic in Chicago all summer long. You just get used to them. Sometimes you wave at them when driving by, while on other days you take a completely different route, avoiding them altogether. At all times, you simply know they are there and you know that at any given moment, three out of the five guys will be standing by the side of the road with seemingly nothing to do,

How Can We Voice Frustration?

while the other two look like prison labor. All five workers, mind you, have orangish-tan skin, and at the end of the day that kind of makes sense. Besides, the only person on the construction crew we really care about is the one holding the sign attached to the seven-foot pole. On one side, it says "stop," while on the other side we read the word "slow." And at the end of the day, that just makes a lot of sense.

Perhaps the best counsel ever given to mankind regarding its tongue lies in that seven-foot sign held by construction crews. Our tongues should be slow to speak and, at other times, we should just stop them from moving at all. Regardless of your view of profanity, there are certain words that simply bother us. Deep within our being, there is some voice that instructs us as to what is good and bad to say out loud. If you are a human being, I will presume that you have ignored those inner voices at times, just as you were driving by the large sign that said "slow," and "stop." May I remind you, then, that fines are doubled in construction areas and that there is a reason the signs are painted some obnoxious orange. So the next time four-letter words come to mind, pause and then stop, or—with the consequences in full view—let them fly for all to admire.

Profanity and New Life

As alluded to earlier, profanity changes things. But then there's another angle. The disciples of Jesus were mostly sailors and I tend to think that their language wasn't quite as sanitary as some Sunday school teachers want to say. But let's not single them out.

Interestingly, women probably get away more with saying the four-letter version of the f-word than they can with the word "feminist" or "feminism," but feminist isn't the only new cuss word that stops churchgoers in their tracks. There are other words like "pro-choice" and "liberal" that also cause murmuring in the room. And on we go trying to find a language that we can use in public that is strong enough to capture emotion and express something deeper inside of us.

A Time to Question Everything

Don't misunderstand me. I am not saying that profanity is the answer for the church. Rather I am saying that a sanitized vocabulary sometimes misses the mark. I am saying that phrases like "gee whiz" aren't strong enough to advocate for the poor, marginalized, or downtrodden. Our own hearts should upset us at times. And being upset shouldn't always look like a sitcom where problems are solved in a half hour with smiles on everyone's faces. When preachers forego preaching the gospel and churches become sanitary clubs for positive thinkers, maybe there's something worth cussing about.

Jesus is amazing yet again as we understand that, during his life as a carpenter, there must have been times when he looked down and saw a splinter sticking out of his hand or maybe he didn't look down and hammered his thumb instead of the nail. Yet, he did all this without sinning. I am so sinful, I almost blurt out profanity in utter amazement at the lack of profanity in the life of Christ.

In the Gospel of Matthew, though, I am struck with the closest thing we have in Scripture to the Messiah blurting out a veritable barrage of bad words. Within less than one chapter of Scripture, Jesus uses the following language to describe the current church leaders in Matthew 23:13-39: "hypocrites. . .you shut the kingdom of heaven in people's faces" (23:13); "Hypocrites. . .you travel across sea and land to make a single proselyte, and when he becomes a proselyte, you make him twice as much a child of hell as yourselves" (23:15); "You blind men. . ..you blind guides. . .you blind Pharisee" (23:19-26).

> You are like whitewashed tombs which outwardly appear beautiful, but within are full of dead people's bones and all uncleanness. So you also outwardly appear righteous to others, but within you are full of hypocrisy and lawlessness. . .you serpents, you brood of vipers, how are you to escape being sentenced to hell? (23:27, 33).

Many of these words are laced with outrage. The language is strong, bold, and unrelenting. And yet, there is no sin here. Jesus, the exact representation of God, the image of the invisible God, speaks truth with not one ounce of sin. Both the outrage and lack of sin must be held in tension. The language of Jesus is strong and, frankly, neither politically correct nor representative of any sensitivity training. The language of Jesus is also charged with emotion and passionate outrage against church leaders who teach something other than the gospel.

When Jesus met the Samaritan woman at the well, he spoke directly, yet minus the outcry. He simply says, "You have had many husbands and the one at home, in your bed, isn't one of them," (John 4:16–18). He speaks directly, gently, firmly. When Peter wants Jesus to reconsider going to the cross, Jesus responds with the words: "Get behind me Satan," (Matt 16:23). Some would call it harsh, but on second glance it's consistent. Jesus reacts very strongly to anyone suggesting another gospel.

Again, I am not advocating for people to start using profanity all over the church. I am simply saying that the Bible teaches a rather startling truth: preachers who teach anything other than the gospel of grace elicit more outrage from Jesus than the outcasts who understand their desperate need for a second chance. This is a new teaching to those who first heard it and it's a fresh perspective for those of us today. Jesus, in this passage of Scripture, seems to have lost patience with church leaders. Most people think the unsanitary people need cleaning up so that they can come to church; Jesus seems to be saying that the dirty ones are those who are welcome to come as they are. God puts it plainly: "man looks at the outward appearance; God looks at the heart" (1 Sam 16:7).

The heart language of Jesus seems different than the heart language of so many of his followers. The expressions of Jesus are at times more raw than we allow in our own lives, and quite possibly his ability to speak the truth in love is what we all admire. At times it seems harsh, while at other times it's the most gracious thing we've ever heard. At all times, his language is something fresh, something new, and something that heals. I spend time on profanity simply to make a sincere point: it is very difficult to speak the truth in love.

A Time to Question Everything

In our age of Twitter rants and social media put-downs, the need to speak the truth in love is more critical than ever. We find too much outrage at times over small, insignificant things. Since we all are imperfect, living in a broken world, how will you speak the truth in love? If we don't learn to do this well, we will continue to have difficulty advancing issues of justice and human rights.

So, how should a Christian lose patience? Maybe that's the wrong question. The question may simply be this: when we lose patience, are we doing so over the right things? Perhaps part of being a new creation is not only caring about new things, but developing a new language that is strong, yet filled with grace, and such a task is impossible without centering on the gospel. If we're honest, most of our Christian lives are pendulums swinging back and forth from the profane to the mundane. The profane allures us with its strength, its raw spontaneity, and protest, but we so often live in the mundane details of life. We fret about what's for dinner, we are discouraged by traffic jams, and we resent having to pay the bills. The mundane doesn't invite us like the profane does. Instead the mundane haunts us and plagues us. We try to escape the mundane and we're taught to avoid the profane, all the while professing to follow a man whose passion changed human history. Many of us are losing patience with ourselves and most of us have already lost patience with the church. Our little journey into profanity has revealed that we are struggling with the words we use to describe the faith we see, feel, and express. We need to work at our words because they truly do matter.

What do you do with your anger? What words do you use when you express frustration with the state of the world? Can you be emotional and speak the truth in love?

8

Who Will Rescue Me?

"God knows better than we do what we need."

—Victor Hugo, *Les Misérables*

ON A FLIGHT FROM Florida to St. Louis, a few years ago, we became one of those families. The ordeal started in Florida when weather delayed our flight for over two hours. We had just visited relatives and my son, who was eighteen months old at the time, seemed to be in a good mood, which meant we were all in a good mood. After the long delay, we boarded the plane and took off. The flight was shorter than our delay, but it was also ninety minutes longer than my son could take. For the last hour and a half of the flight, my toddler screamed as loud as his little body could muster. My wife tried everything. I tried everything. We took turns holding him and we tried to feed him. We stood near the rear bathroom and we tried singing, reading, and whatever else we could think of—nothing worked.

One moment we were putting our heads in our hands and the next, we were trying to smile apologetically at the passengers sitting around us. Finally, I was nearing the end of my sanity. My wife had taken our son to the back toward the restroom to try, yet again, to calm him down. I could feel everyone's eyes looking at us and in particular one woman kept glaring. She finally muttered to me, "Can't you do something?"

"Yes, sorry, we're trying," I said sheepishly.

"Well, try harder," she scolded.

And that was it. Whatever sanity, patience, or anxiety I had tried to maintain or suppress, finally pushed its way from my messed up heart out into the open.

"Ma'am, this is Southwest Airlines. You chose to sit there. No one else made you take that seat," I said, glaring back.

My wife returned shortly and I never looked in the direction of the glaring lady again. So if you are one of those people who love the airplane evangelist stories where you hear about total strangers striking up meaningful, life-changing conversations at 30,000 feet, I am sorry to disappoint. I was overwhelmed, anxious, at wit's end, and the father in one of those families—the ones you don't usually choose to sit next to on a packed airplane. My son was screaming his little head off and nothing was working. I felt helpless, my pride was wounded, and my anxiety was out of control. I simply could not do anything to help the situation.

Have you ever been there? Have you ever come to the realization that you can't do anything to make some situations better? Don't you just want someone or something to rescue you? I felt trapped. The flight was less than three hours, much shorter than the non-stop I have taken from Tokyo to Chicago before, and much shorter than the connecting flights I have taken from London to Ethiopia, but to this day it's one of the longest flights I have ever experienced due not to mileage, but to my own weakness. For the record, my son finally fell asleep when the plane landed and no, I have never seen that glaring lady since.

Questions in the Search

Hamlet famously asked the question, "To be or not to be?," as he contemplated his own life, his father's death, and how he can continue. The rest of Shakespeare's famous play is Hamlet grappling with this very question in relationship to other people. Questions are important because it's so difficult to get the right answers without asking the right questions, and for this reason I find the questions in Romans 7 both fascinating and liberating. One would think that someone like Paul, in the context of acknowledging the ever-present power of sin in his own life, would have more specific questions, but in this letter and in his teaching, he grapples with some intense issues. While many of us typically ask questions like "Why me?" or "What is the reason for that?," Paul asks only four questions over the course of the chapter and they are not the ones I would have asked.

"Do you not know. . .that the law is binding on a person only as long as he lives?" (Rom 7:1). Well, that's not exactly the most comforting thought in the world, is it? Don't worry about the law, it's only binding as long as you live. Yet in context, Paul isn't trying to be trite or negative, but rather he's addressing specific legal concerns. The law, he is saying, is binding for life. Death releases people from legal obligations. Again, this is obvious, but the connection Paul makes catches us a bit off guard.

"Likewise, my brothers, you also have died to the law through the body of Christ, so that you may belong to another, to him who has been raised from the dead, in order that we may bear fruit for God" (Rom 7:4). I am caught off guard because I am suddenly reading about my own death. There have been movies made where one of the characters fakes his or her own death, but Paul isn't talking about a fake death. We're talking about dying to self and rising from the burden of the law itself. The law is good, but only through the lens of grace. Alone, we buckle under its weight. So, I may ask continually, "Who will rescue me?," and the answer is clearly found in the life, death, and resurrection of Jesus. Only Jesus can rescue me from the law and only Jesus liberates me from having to fulfill the law perfectly as long as I live.

"What shall we say then? That the law is sin?" (Rom 7:7a). The next question in the chapter is connected to the first one. If the law is binding as long we walk the earth and that burden is an awful one without Christ, is the law sin? No, the law is not sin, but think of what the law actually does to you. When you are driving down the road and suddenly a police officer appears in your rearview mirror, do you relax, knowing that the authorities are watching your back or do you tense up and try not to make a mistake of any kind? My guess is that you do the latter. You tense up when the "law" follows you down the road for a couple miles. In a real sense, that's what laws do. They appear, they make their presence known, and they remind you of duty, but they cannot deliver you or free you. Is the law, then, sin? If the law is related to such negative emotion isn't it a negative thing?

Our answer must be absolutely not. If you have ever driven a car in another country besides the United States, then you are grateful for the laws in the United States. I remember being in the most amazing traffic jam in Kampala, Uganda, and before my very eyes, cars were actually facing each other on a main road, gridlocked, each driver wanting the other one to move. But it was obvious we were not going to move for quite some time. If you think this is a trite matter and not something worth dwelling on a bit, then take a moment and think about the consequences of all traffic laws in the United States being suspended for one day. One day each year we can just announce that anyone can drive whatever speed they wish and there were no stop signs, traffic lights, or lane markings to obey. Just do whatever you want for one day. How do you think that would go? Personally, I would find a reason to stay home that day. The law isn't sin.

"Did that which is good, then, bring death to me?" (Rom 7:13). Can good things kill you? Again, Paul answers with a resounding no, but you see the personal dilemma, don't you? If the law is good and it's binding as long as I live on earth, then can a good thing bring death to you and to me? At this point, it's worth reflecting a moment on our own tendency to blame everyone but ourselves for things that go wrong in our lives. And Paul is slowly revealing his point by lingering a bit longer on the law than most people would. Think about it, though. If you have ever been pulled over, don't you get a little upset with the cop for following you, a

Who Will Rescue Me?

good, upstanding citizen who rarely does anything wrong? Why can't the cop go catch some real criminals? Why does he have to mess with me?

In a nutshell, that's also our relationship with the law. We'd like to blame it for our trouble, but we can't. The trouble is even more frightening than the law. The trouble is that we want what the law forbids. I want a host of things that are not mine. I am prone to stretching the truth, chasing after other gods, desecrating the Sabbath, and a host of other things. In certain moments and at certain times of the day, I simply want to do my own thing. I don't want to be reminded of law; I just want to do what I want to do.

And here we are suddenly faced with the truth of who we are, particularly if we are confessing believers. We are at war with ourselves because we are at war with sin, which flows out of our hearts or, as Paul puts it, "dwells within me" (7:17). And frankly this is the problem I have with the common phrase "asking Jesus into my heart." Asking Jesus to dwell in my heart is like inviting the President of the United States over to your house for leftovers. If I am going to come face-to-face with Jesus, I want to offer something other than what I usually offer. I want to give him something that I don't normally give. When I recognize Jesus for who he is, I want to give more. Often though, I am reduced to a puddle of tears and emotional rubbish because I don't know what to give that seems good. And this exasperated feeling of wanting to give from the heart but knowing my heart is a mess, drives me to cry out the same question Paul poses next.

"Who will deliver me from this body of death?" (Rom 7:24b). This question is crucial and one you and I must answer at some point. Notice first that the question is not impersonal—it's not a what or a when question, rather it's pointing us to a person. Who will deliver me and who will deliver you from the "sin that dwells within?" For any hope to truly sprout in our being, we need to see the grace of God in the face of Christ.

What then do I do with my anxiety, impatience, foul mouth, and confusion? Who will deliver me from this wretched state that I am so often in? Think about it. You can't blame the driver in front of you for your terrible attitude. You can't blame your spouse or your friends for your language. You can't blame your quick temper or late-night worry on those "bad people." You and I have to reckon with the fact that we need a person to either show us how to keep the law or a person to keep the law on our behalf. We need a person who can show us that the law is good, but limited. Jesus is this person and he isn't an idea, a religious relic, or an ancient artifact. Jesus is alive and real and confronting us with not only the truth about ourselves, but also the grace flowing from God.

Some Questions Answered

Steve is a man I have known since grade school and someone I deeply admire and count as one of my dearest friends. His family always treats me as one of them and he himself has continued to challenge me to be not just a friend, but to be a better one today than I was yesterday. Steve has taught in the Austin neighborhood of Chicago for many years now and I admire him deeply for being an exceptional math teacher. I look up to him in many respects and am grateful for him. Yet to me, his heroism isn't found in his working in inner-city Chicago, nor in the way he cares for his beautiful family. To me, Steve has always pointed me toward Jesus in some way or another and that's as heroic as it gets. Why? Because as much as I love Steve, he's still a man caught in the same muck and mire as I am, and while a good many people would point to him and comment on his sacrificial work, Jesus comes to both Steve and I with the message that it's okay to be weak. It's okay to be weak, because Jesus has our back.

This freedom to be weak is, to me, what it means to be justified by faith alone. I don't have to defend myself or stick up for myself, Jesus will do that for me. You see now why life is so messy, don't you? You and I must constantly remind ourselves to relax and let the gift of faith be enough to guard and guide us.

I am prone, though, to be not only weak, but melancholy and downright depressed at times, both with myself and with the state of things. I have always resonated with the lost son (more famously known as the Prodigal Son) and his rehearsal of the phrase, "I am not worthy," as he headed for home because he was weak, low, and had no idea where else to go. Paul Miller is so helpful when he writes,

> In the parable about the Lost Son, Jesus tells us what to say when we come home to God. Along with the lost son, you could say to your heavenly Father, "I've lived in your world but ignored you. I've done what felt good and it hasn't worked. I've not loved the way Jesus loved. I often put up a good front, yet there are those secret moments of despair that I tell no one about. I am empty. So now I come home asking your forgiveness. I lay my life down in your strong arms. I surrender. Thank you for welcoming me home."[1]

You can picture the lost son almost collapsing into the arms of someone stronger, someone whose hug won't crush him; it's a Father's embrace that protects him and lets him know that it's okay to be weak. Paul Miller concludes with these words:

> Love didn't just walk among us. He can indwell us. Jesus repeatedly told people, "In me you'll find your deepest needs met—your need for forgiveness, love, hope, belonging, and purpose. I am what you've always been looking for."[2]

When I was on the Southwest flight with my son screaming his head off, I fought against my weakness. I wanted to be seen as a good parent, a good neighbor, and an exemplary father and passenger. I didn't want to be one of those families who no one wants to sit next to. Rather, I wanted to be the family everyone wants to sit with because our family wasn't weak, we were in control. We had read the parenting books, we had taken the necessary steps, and made the necessary arrangements. We came to that situation prepared to give it our best—the problem was this: our best

---

1. Miller, *Love Walked among Us*, 253.
2. Ibid., 253.

A Time to Question Everything

sometimes isn't good enough. And if you're a follower of Christ, that's okay. Jesus has got your back.

Let's fast forward to another Southwest Airlines flight (and yes, this is as close as it gets to product placement in this book), only this time we were flying from Birmingham, Alabama, to Phoenix, Arizona. I am sitting next to the window, my pre-teen son sat in the middle, and a young woman (I say young because she's close to my age, mid-to-late thirties) is on the aisle. On this flight we hit a bit of turbulence, but my son doesn't notice. He's too busy eating his snack and reading his book. He's not screaming his head off at all. In fact, the turbulence bothers me more than it does him.

Suddenly, the woman on the aisle turns and begins to strike up small talk. She's a nurse, it turns out, and she misses her own children. As the flight continues, my son and the nurse talk back and forth and then the nurse suggests they watch a cartoon on her iPod together. She asks me if it's okay and I nod. For the rest of the flight, my son and the nurse share snacks, cartoons, and laughter. Then, when the flight lands, she thanks me. And I smile to myself as I am a slow learner, but the picture hits me clearly and with force. The nurse thanked me, the father, for time with my son. I wanted to say, "Are you kidding? You should have been on that other flight!" Then another thought struck me when I thought about the glaring woman on the other flight: "Where has this nurse been all our lives?"

But, by God's grace, I said nothing. I simply got off the plane and thanked God for the nudge to remember that spending time with Jesus is always something to be thankful for. I should probably turn to the Father more often to say thanks for letting me eat and laugh with his Son. His Son, after all, is our only hope for being rescued from ourselves and this fractured world.

What do you need to notice today that you didn't yesterday because you were too preoccupied with rehearsed answers instead of deeper questions?

A month or so after moving to the Kansas City area, I became very ill with what turned out to be a nasty bacterial infection. I

Who Will Rescue Me?

spent one afternoon hooked up to an IV, dehydrated and exhausted. After getting an antibiotic injection, the doctor said, "you're free to go home." I said nothing. I took a few minutes to pull myself up from the bed and then stumbled behind my wife and children who were patiently waiting to drive me home. My kindergarten-age daughter could have easily knocked me over; I was very weak. So, what does a weak person do with freedom? I did exactly what the doctor told me to do; I went home to rest.

I felt no anxiety at all and I felt no impulse to hide my sad state of health. I just didn't care. I was weak and was fine with it. I just wanted to go home and rest. Interestingly, I also felt an amazing freedom. I had a piece of paper in my hand for a prescription which allowed me to not only get some drugs, but it also showed everyone who walked by that I was weak, sick, and getting help. Think about this for a moment and see if you agree. Do you feel more freedom when you are weak or when you are strong? Of course, we can debate the nuances of the question, but I don't think you or I should answer quickly. Our knee-jerk reaction is to confuse freedom and independence. In the United States, we declare our independence every July and celebrate our freedom from every other nation. But, freedom is more than simply a democratic republic and more than possessing power. It has to be more because Paul wrote these words while living under Caesar's rule: "Therefore, there is now no condemnation for those who are in Christ Jesus" (Rom 8:1). And if you and I cannot be condemned, then we are free. For emphasis, Paul reiterates his point later in the same chapter with these words:

> If God is for us, who can be against us? He who did not spare his own Son but gave him up for us all, how will he not also with him graciously give us all things? Who shall bring any charge against God's elect? It is God who justifies. Who is to condemn?" (Rom 8:31b–34a)

If you've ever seen something grand or beautiful or awe-inspiring that made you stop in your tracks, then now's the time to do the same thing. Don't miss the shift from the end of Romans 7 to the end of Romans 8. We have just gone from asking "Who

A Time to Question Everything

will deliver me from this body of death?" to "Who shall bring any charge against me?" You and I, drunk on grace, are free, and since we are justified by the work of Christ, we are weak, wounded, sick, and sore. But instead of carrying a prescription, we're carrying the promises of Jesus around and the words to us are the same: "now go home and rest."

The gospel is good news that sets us free. There are no shackles on us, so the hymn writer can say with confidence, "my chains fell off, I rose, went forth, and followed thee."[3] I love the truth of this in the gospel and I am scared to believe it. If I believe it, then what will I do with my anxiety, regret, and self-hatred? If it's okay to be weak, then why do I fight it? It's easier to be chained to something, because then I can blame the chains or the prison doors or the warden of the prison or a host of other factors. But if the chains are off, I may only be left with my unbelief. This is the negative side of things.

What happens, though, if I begin to actually believe this stuff? Steve Brown is correct when he writes,

> It ought to be simple. If Jesus said we're free, we ought to accept his declaration at face value and run with it. It ought to help us define ourselves. But it doesn't. Christians will do almost anything to get away from the simple meaning of the word and the wonderful experience of freedom. Something about freedom scares us to death. We continue in our bondage—and that is a major tragedy. It is a tragedy because Christ went to so much trouble to set us free. It is a tragedy because there is so much more to being a Christian than obeying rules, doing religious things and being "nice."[4]

The statement of the doctor is haunting: "now go home and rest." When I am weak, sure, that's an appealing thought, but I am often under the delusion that I am strong, self-sufficient, and ready to take on whatever comes my way. I forget the questions of Romans 7 and remember only the ones at the end of Romans 8 and in

3. Wesley, "And Can it Be," 455.
4. Brown, *Scandalous Freedom*, 7.

doing so, miss the point. I remember that no one will separate me from the love of God. I also know that I don't always feel like I'm going to make it. How can we live in freedom?

I am free because I know that I am not the strong one. I am not the one who will rescue anyone from sin. I am in trouble if Jesus leaves me to myself. I wonder—does any of this resonate with you? I ask because I struggle so often to truly grasp it and hold it close.

I am free to love my children without grading their behavior or setting myself up as anything but human. I love them from a weak and low position already. I am free to love other people who may not love me in return, because their lack of love doesn't enslave me. Truly my debts have been cast on Christ, so I must and shall go free. There is no other way to live as a Christian. If I want to live in a way that is against the Christian faith, then give me a bunch of rules to follow, point out my flaws regularly, and tell me that I need to be good, nice, and upright like those other people. Tell me often what I do wrong and then withhold praise when I do well, then I may be like everyone else who has no idea what grace is about. Remind me often that I don't measure up and throw in a few jabs about things I did long ago. Steve Brown continues, "Freedom threatens religious people because it takes away their leverage and makes it more difficult for them to maintain control."[5]

My uncle used to be a prison guard at the Joliet State Penitentiary outside of Chicago. I recall some of his stories and one thing struck me—even murderers, rapists, and serial killers talk about getting out.

All human beings, whether convicted criminals or confessing Christians, all move when the prison doors are flung open. Freedom is more than a declaration, it's also motivation. Jesus releases us to go somewhere. Once we understand that we are free to go home and rest, we may begin to understand that we are also free to move toward participating in the restoration of all things. Let me put it another way. Once we recognize that we are part of the problem, we can now be freed to be part of the solution. The same

---

5. Ibid., 19.

freedom in Christ that causes us to embrace our weakness liberates us to also to embrace his strength.

And it's these wants and desires that are revealed when we embrace our freedom in Christ. Now that you're free and on the move, where do you want to go? What do you want to do? How we answer these questions reveals not only our wants, but also how seriously we have taken the gospel. After coming face-to-face with Christ and experiencing the grace of God, have our wants and desires changed at all?

I have seen and heard many preachers and teachers get all lathered up as they outline the need for all God's people to go to the mission field or get out of their comfort zone or go out to change the world. Andy Crouch is instructive when he writes,

> Changing the world sounds grand, until you consider how poorly we do even at changing our own little lives. On a daily basis we break our promises, indulge our addictions and rehearse old fantasies and grudges that even we know we'd be better off without. We have changed less about ourselves than we would like to admit. Who are we to charge off to change the world?[6]

One answer to Crouch's question is that we are no big deal. We are people who live in the tension of our wants and needs and we so often want sinful things as well as sacred things. We are often stuck trying to make up our minds between living in grace and living under crushing rules. We want the world to change before we do, not because we're lacking movement, but because we believe that once we make a declaration to follow Jesus, then we somehow deserve more, are entitled to more, so therefore we demand more from the world in which we live. Deep down, many of us believe that we're owed something for believing in truth, but how messed up is that? If we pause to take a deep breath from our self-obsession, then Crouch's question humbles us and doesn't seem so far off.

---

6. Crouch, *Culture Making*, 200.

Who Will Rescue Me?

Yet, there's another way to answer the question. And here is where it gets really messy. Will the world really change any other way? God is mysterious and majestic. God knows more than us, loves more than us, and forgives more than us without question. And part of God's mystery and majesty is the fact that he decides to use sinful, fallible, messed up people to spread the message of his grace. God sent his only Son to die, rise again, and advocate on our behalf to set a people free to live and love in his grace. In fact, Acts 17:6 chronicles an amazing phrase that is both instructive as well as intimidating. We're told that "These men who have turned the world upside down have come here also" to presumably do the same. You see the movement in the verse, don't you? "These men . . .have come here," is a very different picture than "these men stayed over there." These changed, free men have come toward us, they didn't stay in their church clusters, church buildings, or church groups. These men who have been transformed by grace are now coming toward us, with fear and trembling maybe, but with freedom and purpose for sure. What will other people do when an unleashed group of people starts coming toward them in humility, love, and grace? Eugene Peterson, in *The Message*, writes, "The Word became flesh and blood, and moved into the neighborhood."[7] Jesus himself models true freedom when he, by choice, leaves the privileges of heaven to experience the perils of Earth. Jesus moves toward you and I with a freedom that baffles the mind but displays his mission. And it's in his freedom that his death and resurrection mean so much. If Jesus is forced or coerced or duped into a sacrificial life, then we're not impressed.

Peterson reminds us that suddenly the neighborhoods began to change because changed people moved in next door. And again, we're back to our life of wants and needs. Do you want to move toward other people or do you need to move toward other people? I am stuck many days, knowing full well that I would like to avoid people, avoid pain, and stay, not necessarily safe, but simply to myself. Then I can't be blamed or shamed into thinking I had anything to do with the demise of that city or that neighborhood or

---

7. Peterson, *Message (Remix)*, 1558.

A Time to Question Everything

those people. If I stay away long enough, then I can fool myself into believing that I have no responsibility for my fellow man or the common good. Rather, I can simply live a quiet life, keeping to myself and making various critical comments when I witness something go horribly wrong. The gospel, though, moves me toward other people. In his grace, I enter into another person's pain and am drawn to our common bond as redeemed image-bearers of God.

The vast majority of criticism is done either behind someone's back or at a safe distance. Instead of entering into a potentially messy situation, people stay away and create a new mess (gossip) under the illusion of safety. In short, he or she refuses to embrace the mess that so often characterizes human relationships and instead potentially creates a new mess through gossip or slander. What would happen though if we embraced the mess that is authentic love? To follow Jesus means following a man who entered into a lot of messy situations, not because he went looking for trouble, but because he went looking for you and for me in a fallen world.

Entering in to the mess of life happens when we are free to do so, loving people from our own weak position, moving toward needy people. We are free to love because we don't have to fix anyone, rescue anyone, or judge anyone. Instead, we just have to "move into the neighborhood." Being unchained simply prepares us to be unleashed. The movement that happens once we've experienced grace is then not a movement of our own doing. Rather we are suddenly swept up in a sacred movement of God.

Jeff Imbach makes a profound statement though when he writes that "people don't want us to change because they'll have to change, too. The rules in the relationship are changed when we change and grow."[8] In other words, when the gospel transforms our hearts and makes us new creations, we disrupt the status quo that is stuck on following rules and creating man-made, self-exalting, insulated lives that retreat from chaos into the well-ordered life of our choosing. To put it another way, grace makes a mess.

---

8. Imbach, *River Within*, 180.

Who Will Rescue Me?

Imbach also says "as people are set free to be passionate about life, often they choose something unexpected, something truly fresh that becomes a wonderful gift to the world. As they find small ways to say yes to the life inside them, their whole countenance brightens, and they begin to move into a sense of power and freedom."[9] Passionate people, then, embrace the mess in life because they just might do something unexpected, such as pack up the family and move to Africa to serve the poor. Other people may be set free to quit their Fortune 500 position to preach the gospel. Some people will stay at the Fortune 500 company but will turn down a promotion to spend more time with family. When's the last time grace caused you to do something unexpected?

People changed by grace begin to break our paradigms for how life is to be lived and are consistently open to what is new because God has given them a new heart and a new vision of a new heaven and a new Earth. Once the old paradigm of self-promoting, rules-based living is broken, people are set free to live in the moment and, to a watching world, this begins to look reckless and messy. Instead of slowing down or retreating into a monastery or countryside castle, grace-shaped, grace-focused people suddenly start moving into the neighborhood, coming ever closer to the idols we clutch with modern minds and postmodern hearts. Our status quo lives are threatened by grace and, in the eyes of God, that's fine. In fact, God may just be saying that it's about time the world is turned upside down again. At the very least, shouldn't this cause us to rethink how we live on planet Earth?

9. Ibid., 179.

9

Is God Satisfied?

"I'm not 'happy' but I'm not unhappy about it."

—Alan Bennett, *The History Boy*

As you think about your own wants and desires, does it ever occur to you that God may have some wants and desires as well? Let's put it another way. Is God satisfied? Is God satisfied with his existence? Is God satisfied with you and with me? How we answer the question is important because it reveals either our confidence in his grace or our concern over his condemnation; we are either looking upward in worship or over our shoulder in worry.

The striking thing though is that perhaps we don't believe there was ever any wrath to be satisfied. Maybe you think God never gets angry. After all, that's the Old Testament version of God, not the one Jesus speaks of to the outcasts and misfits in the New Testament. At least, that's what you say to yourself in the hope that the guilt in your heart will go away.

God wants a relationship with us but isn't satisfied to leave us sitting in the muck and mire of our own sinful lives without a way out of the mess we've made. As a loving parent, God isn't satisfied

Is God Satisfied?

to leave his children alone. So if you're dissatisfied with your own flaws, depression, anxiety, impatience, and imperfections, then you're in good company. God isn't satisfied with his people being left in a rebellious, rotten state either. Yet God is satisfied with[1] what Jesus has done and, remarkably, God is satisfied with our trusting in Jesus alone for our salvation, healing, rescue, and redemption. And bigger than the fact that Jesus has accomplished all this is the truth that God is completely and totally satisfied with what Jesus has done. Why is this so difficult for us to grasp in the core of our being? Imagine if this truth worked its way in to the fabric of who we are like a new strand of DNA that would alter our chemical make-up and genetic code. God is satisfied with what Jesus has done. Rejoice and be glad in it. Get over your pettiness and work through your shame, God is not ashamed of you even if your faith is the size of a mustard seed. Of course, if you have no faith and you simply shrug and ignore God, then two things are likely true: this life is satisfying to you and the evil all around you has numbed you to what is good, true, and beautiful, and you may think that this life is all there is, so be happy until you die. My only question is this: Deep down are you truly content and satisfied with where you are and where you are headed? And if so, are you content to ignore the possibility that there is a God who isn't satisfied with your life until you have a good, long, hard look at Jesus?

When God Sees Us

What do we all do when we look into mirrors? Don't we all do one of two things? Either we primp and prepare to look at ourselves or we try to fix something that we see about ourselves. Seriously, take time to confess the truth. If you looked in a mirror this morning, did you try to fix your hair, clear up some acne, or address the redness, sleep, and lines in and around your eyes? After you addressed these issues, did you then look in the mirror again, in the hope that something had changed (for the better, of course)? Let's then add to the equation the myriad advertisements that show us how we should look, the internal knowledge that we don't look like we thought we would at this age, and the nagging feeling that someone has noticed that one freckle, mole, or gray hair that we've tried to hide, and we are beginning to understand a bit of the insecurity in which we all live. And if this is the way we live in front of ourselves and one another, what happens when we are confronted with the gaze of a perfect and all-knowing God?

One day, while walking into a shopping mall, my six-year-old daughter, holding my hand, pointed and said in a loud voice "Oh, look at that man smoking. . .that's so disgusting!" Of course, the man, a retail worker puffing away on his cigarette break, was horrified (and so was I a bit at the volume of my daughter's voice). I gave an apologetic look to the man as we walked into the store and tried to explain to my daughter that pointing at people and saying words like "disgusting" is a bad idea. The man put his cigarette out almost immediately and he shuffled back to work without looking at my daughter again. Our family smiles often at our daughter's gift in pointing out the flaws of others (because she's little and cute, but I am sure the smiles have an expiration date) and on this one day, I wondered if the smoker reacted more to the innocence of a cute little girl than he did the finger pointing and the "that's disgusting." In fact, it's a small picture of how we all react, isn't it? Typically it isn't what we're doing, but who notices what we're doing that is the issue.

Jerram Barrs notes that "All over the world there is the knowledge that our present condition is one of alienation and rebellion, that we are not all we should be. . ...All over the world, there is a longing for this brokenness to be set right. . .,"[1] yet I think you already know that. In the recesses of the human heart, I suspect many of us know that human beings let us down. But do we think God lets us down? Does God disappoint you? If so, why do you think that is? Perhaps it's worth looking beyond our own situation to understand God a bit better.

God doesn't just see you, He sees all of us. He isn't just interested in your life or my life, but he is interested in the big picture of all of our lives. God doesn't compartmentalize humanity, like

---

1. Barrs, *Echoes of Eden*, 75.

Is God Satisfied?

we all do. He doesn't see Presbyterians, Anglicans, Methodists, and Catholics; God sees his people and his people know his voice. Sure, God relates to us on an individual basis where we pray alone and cry out for help, but God is moving history and not simply motivating a person here or there. Like it or not, we are part of something bigger than ourselves, and God is fashioning a people for a new heaven and a new Earth. When God sees us, he notices the warts and all, that is true, but God sees us with a multi-dimensional eye that knows the end of the story. We're invited to believe that Jesus has ushered into this world a new way of living, loving, and learning. Until we embrace this invitation to something new, God will be all-sufficient, but not satisfied. God, in his son Jesus, asks us to repent and believe, not an old story, but a new teaching.

As God sees us, we are in need of a new life, since we are dead in sin and often blind to the work of a loving Creator who is satisfied with the work of Jesus and is satisfied with, not our works, but our faith. Our small faith in a great and glorious God is satisfying all the way round. John Stott summarizes things succinctly when he writes,

> God declares us righteous through the death of his Son, by faith only, so that our justification is both instantaneous and complete. But God makes us righteous through the indwelling of his Spirit, by faith and works, so that our sanctification is both gradual and incomplete.[2]

We are works in progress, true, but on the basis of the finished work of Christ. Without the satisfying work of Jesus, there is no promise fulfilled and progress to be made because Christ is the foundation for what lies ahead. Without standing on the shoulders of what Jesus has done, we stand before God appealing to the unsatisfying work of someone other than Jesus. And ask any human parent what they think of you ignoring their only son and then appealing to their goodness on the basis of the fact that at least you paid attention to your own? How is that honestly going to work?

---

2. Stott, *Evangelical Truth*, 80.

A Time to Question Everything

God, at the bare minimum, wants us to take his only Son seriously before we move on to anything else.

When We See God

Perhaps part of our anxiety, impatience, and frustrations in life are linked not only to the daily reality of problems and imperfections, but also a persistent attitude that we've got God figured out and that he is unhappy, picky, and well, a more powerful version of us. Don't disagree with this too quickly. Think about it.

Have you ever felt that God doesn't like you, isn't interested in your life, and is mysteriously unable to help you? Or worse, that he doesn't want to help you because you're not worth it? In our efforts to make sure we retain both the sinfulness of humanity and the holiness of God in our theology, we often fall off the edge on either side. For example, even the rapist, child molester, and man guilty of the torture and slaughter of families in wartime is created in the image of God. The imprint of deity isn't placed on people after years of behaving a certain way or believing certain creedal statements. Every single little baby born into this world bears the image of God as certainly and as surely as he or she has a genetic code or fingerprint.

Yet when we talk of the sinfulness of humanity we make sure people understand that they are flawed and we emphasize their inability to save themselves, but we do so in a way that is often less than human. Using Romans 3 to tell someone that they are worthless is not doctrinal truth; it's damaging trash. People don't attain worth suddenly upon their confession of faith. No, people are born with dignity and value, and they reflect incredible potential communicated through a loving and careful Creator. There is a mystery to the bad behavior of some people, but this mystery does not diminish the good creation of God. This is important because if we feel worthless and less than human, then our view of God becomes less than divine. And this leads us to falling off the edge on the other side.

Is God Satisfied?

God is holy and there is a purity that God reflects, a mystery, a majesty, and an awe that we must take seriously and humbly receive. But this doesn't mean that God is inaccessible, distant, or detached. Holiness means "set apart," not "set against" or "set in opposition to" or even "set aside." When we say God is holy, we want to respect God's power, knowledge, presence, and purity, but we want to do so in a way that retains God's personal and beautiful presence. Living in this gap between our image-bearing selves and the God whose image we bear is a daily part of the life we live. Coming to grips with our human dignity and our human inability is an important matter and something we have to work on. Part of coming to grips with this tension is also recognizing that God is inseparably holy and loving, just and gracious, personal and mysterious. God is knowable, yet beyond comprehension. In short, God is God, and we are not.

To Be Known or Noticed?

While watching a public television news program, I nodded as a social commentator made the statement that we are now living in a world that doesn't do conversations well. Instead, we have digressed into personal broadcasting more than personal relationships. I fear this has spilled into our understanding of how we relate to God. Would you rather have God know you or notice you? It's not an easy question, but it's a revealing one, isn't it?

Let's reflect on the second option first. If God didn't know us well, but noticed us often, what would change? I fear that we don't really want to be known by God and thus we don't really want to be known by other people. Instead, we want God's attention and, subsequently, we want to be noticed by other people. This has translated itself into a myriad of online social networking opportunities, where each of us is able to broadcast ourselves the way we want. In other words, we rather like the option of controlling what others notice or know about us. This isn't love and this isn't Christian and this isn't the way God works.

A Time to Question Everything

God knows us and desires to know us, and then he commands that we love each other. To love well, we need to know each other well. This takes time, but it will also involve seeing things that many would like to have hidden. To be truly known is far more important than being noticed online, and it's much different than Facebook or Twitter, where we have the power to draw attention to only certain aspects of our lives. Parker Palmer convicts us and teaches us when he writes that

> The failure of modern knowledge is not primarily a failure in our ethics, in the application of what we know. Rather, it is the failure of our knowing itself to recognize and reach for its deeper source and passion, to allow love to inform the relations that our knowledge creates—with ourselves, with each other, and with the whole animate and inanimate world.[3]

Love doesn't motivate us to broadcast ourselves on the web (self-love perhaps does) because love seeks to know and understand. Palmer concludes with these words:

> Curiosity and control create a knowledge that distances us from each other and the world, allowing us to use what we know as a plaything and to play the game by our own self-serving rules. But a knowledge that springs from love will implicate us in the web of life; it will wrap the knower and the known in compassion, in a bond of awesome responsibility as well as transforming joy; it will call us to involvement, mutuality, and accountability.[4]

God isn't satisfied to notice our existence; he seeks relationship and initiates within us a craving for intimacy that cannot be quenched by our own attempts to be noticed. So why do even Christians clamor for attention and relevance in a world more obsessed with being noticed than known? Perhaps it's because even Christians have bought into the lie that being noticed is as important as being known. Another more frightening idea is this: maybe

---

3. Palmer, *To Know as We are Known*, 9.
4. Ibid., 9.

Is God Satisfied?

we really are control freaks and we rather like the distance that control offers as opposed to the closeness and revealing knowledge that love demands. Personal broadcasting offers us attention and positive feedback but won't challenge or change us. On the other hand, personal relationships bound together in love, motivated by love, and grounded in compassion will force us to repent, forgive, and confront our assumptions, prejudices, and understanding. In short, love will change us and, since God is love, we would rather be noticed and left alone more often than we would like to admit. Jesus, though, comes to us and disrupts our status quo visions of others and versions of reality, and asks us to consider a different way of relating to God and people. In Christ, we embrace the disrupting truth that God didn't just notice a lost and hurting people; God *so loved* a lost and hurting people.

So, is God satisfied? The answer lies in something deeper. God isn't satisfied to leave us the way we are, but God is satisfied with Jesus, our small faith, and with love taking precedence over distance and control. To be Christian means to seek something that will change us, and many people ignore or avoid this truth. To be Christian doesn't mean we put a Christian label on the things we like, the G-rated moments of life, or good manners. Instead, to be Christian is to be known by a God who will disrupt our lives until we are transformed into a new creation. In our search for a truly Christian life, we wrestle with this truth: Christians are people who are willing and ready to change. If you don't want to change or feel like you don't need to, then Christianity isn't for you. But, if you're willing to admit that your life could use a spiritual awakening, Jesus invites you to sit down at a table with living bread and fine wine. Eat and drink your fill, because the feast has only just started and the meal is a blessed sign of things to come.

10

Are Your Plans Working?

> "You know what I've noticed? Nobody panics when things go 'according to plan,' even if the plan is horrifying!"
>
> —*The Joker, Dark Knight*

BLOOD-STAINED GLASS LITTERED THE room and the sound of the crash of the window left us all with a flurry of questions. Soon flashing police lights swallowed up the darkness and the search was on. Following clues left behind, the police eventually caught up with the young man who had marched up to our large family room window that faced the street and punched through it in a fit of rage. When asked why he did it, he replied that his girlfriend had just broken up with him and he just needed to hit something.

I am going to tell you something very important, so pay attention: your plans may fail today. Whatever you planned for your day may not come true. Whatever you have planned for your week may not work out very well. You may even pause right now and sigh and mutter under your breath that your plans keep getting messed up and that if I only knew half of your story, I'd be shocked.

Are Your Plans Working?

Well, if your plans have ever been screwed up, keep reading and pay attention, because this isn't just about you or your plans.

When I was finishing high school, a friend and I had just completed a round of golf and were heading home in his blue Toyota. As typical teens, we talked about nothing in particular or at least nothing memorable. As my friend drove on, the blacktop road suddenly turned to gravel. As the surface beneath the car changed and became unsettled, my friend applied the brake and honestly, that's all I remember until we stopped spinning. The car swerved out of control, hitting an embankment, and flipping over, so that we came to a halt upside down. Glass shattered, metal bent and mangled, and two young men scrambled to figure out if they were going to be able to get out in one piece. This was not the ride home we had planned.

So, what do you do when life throws you a curve and upends you? Have you ever felt out of control and like things are suddenly upside down? I recall broken glass on my lap, unbuckling my seat belt to see if I could move, and I remember phone calls to parents and the police. I remember that it did not take long for us to suddenly be upside down in a moving vehicle and I remember being scared at how quickly things spun out of control. Even routine life doesn't slow down, but when unexpected, unwanted, uninvited change comes, things seem to move even faster and suddenly the ground beneath us seems to shift and we wonder if anyone is in control at all.

Our Good Plans are Not God's Redemptive Plan

My life has not turned out the way I had anticipated or planned. Some of this is surely my fault. I have made my share of bad decisions, life-altering choices, and just plain dumb moves. And my guess is, so have you. In addition though, I have had some rather good ideas that have not come to fruition. Nothing earthshaking, but the glass isn't half empty.

Nevertheless, I have been let down by people who said they would tell the truth, who said they could keep a secret, and who

A Time to Question Everything

said they loved me. Family members have said or done hurtful things and friends have forgotten to return calls or even show up. In short, I thought things would turn out differently, not because I deserved it, but because I had plans.

The Christian life is not about what we have planned to do, but what God has planned to do through the person, work, and teachings of Jesus. The Christian life is not about getting our way but following the Way. Imagine a world in which every person had their plans turn out the way that he or she wanted. What a mess! What happens in a baseball game when the pitcher plans to strike out the batter who is planning to jack the ball over the fence? What happens when a young girl plans to make the ballet company, but the hours and hours of hard work are not rewarded? What happens when a family plans a vacation, dependent on the husband's job, but that income suddenly vanishes with phrases like "layoff" and "new directions?" Inherently, we know that someone's plans must fail, we just don't like it when those plans originated in our own heart. If we're honest, most of us believe our plans should succeed.

Our plans are sometimes subjected to unexpected, uninvited, and unwanted change because we simply have no patience to see them through, not only ignoring wise counsel but pushing a different timetable as well. We sabotage our own good ideas with what Paul, in his letter to the Galatians, calls "the desires of the flesh" (Gal 5:17). In fact, ponder this thought: "the desires of the flesh are against the Spirit, and the desires of the Spirit are against the flesh, for these are opposed to each other, *to keep you from doing the things you want to do*," (Gal 5:17, emphasis added). This underscores not only the importance of prayer and compassion in the life of the Christian, but humility and listening ears.

Now note that I have not said our plans are not necessarily bad. Quite the contrary. Some of us have very good ideas and well-thought-out plans. The point here is not to insult your intelligence nor discourage dreams, but as a car begins to pull to one side or the other when the alignment falters, so our lives seem to be tossed around on the waves of our agendas, appointments, broken promises, and altered plans. Although we try to steer effectively

Are Your Plans Working?

through unexpected change, if we are not aligned properly, we will find ourselves stranded on the side of the road or exhausted from the fight to just keep driving. Sometimes the energy it takes just to push through unwanted change causes us to lose hope or lose sight of the fact that God's redemptive plan truly is worth more reflection. In fact, until we truly experience deep disappointment in having our own plans changed or altered, we may not really appreciate the beauty and grandeur of what God is doing all around us.

God, though, isn't just doing something in our world and around us; he is constantly working behind the scenes, inside of us. What we plan is often what we want while what God plans is what is best. A critical question haunts us: Do we ever want what God wants?

Have you ever been in a conversation with someone where the subject turned from something light to something heavy? One minute you're talking about sports or the weather, and the next minute the issue of genocide in Rwanda comes up or the death of a loved one finds its way into the exchange. Two things normally happen: first, the atmosphere becomes weighty and serious; secondly, things slow down. The same happens when we go from shallow to deep.

If you have ever gone diving underwater, you know that the deeper you swim, the more pressure you feel, particularly in your head. The same is true when we talk of things that matter more than the weather or last night's television sitcom. There is a certain pressure that builds up and it must be addressed. Divers know that they can only continue to go deeper if they have the proper training and equipment. In other words, good divers prepare to go deep. If the diver is unprepared, then he or she will retreat to shallow water as quickly as possible.

I fear many of us are inexperienced divers and are often ill prepared to go deep. The apostle Peter tells us that we should always be "prepared to make a defense to anyone who asks you for a reason for the hope that is in you; yet do it with gentleness and respect" (1 Pet 3:15). Being prepared, though, takes work and training and often it even takes making mistakes.

The same man who denied Jesus three times writes that we should be prepared to give an answer for what we hope in. You get the irony, don't you? But you should also see the grace of God in these words. Peter did stand up at Pentecost and gave an amazing account that was so deep and thoughtful that God used him to bring three thousand people to a saving knowledge of Christ. Peter knows that these are life and death matters. And it's the gravity that often keeps us from asking the right questions or pursuing satisfying answers. Gravity, by definition, keeps us grounded. Gravity can be sobering not because it pulls us down, but because it reminds us of our own limitations.

From One Life to Another

So far in this book I have tried not simply to describe a certain life, but to invite you to dwell in it, sit with it a while, and perhaps look at both my life and your own life in a new way. Did you see yourself in the story or did you feel anything at all about parts of my own story? How did you react? Did anything get under your skin? What emotions did you feel? I am only asking because it's now time to leave that life behind for something better. The gospel invites you to something better.[1]

Jesus calls us to rethink our lives and consider something better. We are invited to leave one life (which is really no life at all) for a completely new life (which to the world *looks* like no life at all, where dying to self and trusting in Christ alone, betting the farm on grace alone, feels like death).

Dan Allender and Tremper Longman, in their book entitled *Bold Love*, write that

---

1. Staff members at World Harvest Mission, now called Serge (www.serge.org) have continually reminded me of this truth. The gospel always invites us to something better. See also their courses entitled "Gospel Transformation" and "Sonship" for fuller treatments of a new life.

Are Your Plans Working?

> Our love ought to draw others to a taste of life that satisfies like no other, and our strength ought to warn others that pursuit of a false god leads to an abyss that will eventually violate and destroy their soul...giving them a taste of life that both draws them to hunger for what they've been created for and repels them from what would destroy their life. In essence, bold love is a unique blend of invitation and warning—a pull toward life and push away from death.[2]

Jesus invited a woman who was caught in adultery to a new life with both an invitation and a warning. First, he invites the woman with these words, "Woman, where are they? Has no one condemned you?" (John 8:10). The woman replies that indeed no one has condemned her. Jesus repeats the invitation by saying, "Neither do I condemn you," (John 8:11) and then states "go, and from now on sin no more." Jesus reiterates the invitation, then warns her, all the while inviting her to something better. In Romans 8:1 we read, "There is therefore now no condemnation for those who are in Christ Jesus." In Christ, we have been invited to lose one life and gain another. Yet we cannot simply skip past the invitation and the warning. As we seek a new life that sets us free from anxiety, impatience, or control, we must understand that both invitation and warning are linked. Indeed, Jesus invites us to something better; he comes to us full of grace and truth (John 1:14). The warning is this: to embrace this invitation, you and I will have to give some things up. We cannot accept both the invitation to something new while steadfastly embracing something old. It's akin to swallowing vitamins and antibiotics and then chasing them down with rat poison. We would be quite sick despite good things going inside us. We need to get to the point of taking the vitamins and antibiotics without swallowing the poison too.

Francis Schaeffer puts it this way:

> The true Christian life, true spirituality, does not just mean that we have been born again. It must begin there, but it means much more than that. It does not mean only

---

2. Allender and Longman, *Bold Love*, 211.

that we are going to be in heaven. It does mean that, but it means much more than that. The true Christian life, true spirituality in the present life, means more than being justified and knowing that I am going to heaven..... Our desire must be for a deeper life.[3]

We have been invited to something deeper. We have been invited to something better.

---

3. Schaeffer, *True Spirituality*, 14.

11

Faith Isn't Normal, is It?

"Funny how the nature of a normal day is the first memory to fade."
—Lionel Shriver, *We Need to Talk About Kevin*

"And tonight's top story. . .everything is normal. . ." says the CNN anchor from another planet. Normal isn't newsworthy; normal isn't something anyone pays money to see. So why aren't more people interested in faith? Doesn't the world yet know that faith in God isn't normal?

When you were young, did you put your faith in God or in the God that people told you about? There's a difference and you know that inherently. Simply put, faith is trust. Faith is believing that it's okay to sit in the empty chair because you are sure it will hold you. On the one hand, you can trust an idea or you can trust the person who shared the idea, but on the other hand, you trust something that is more personal. Faith in things we cannot see isn't natural or normal. From an early age, we trust the people we see. The Bible asks us not simply to believe, but to trust that which is often not visible.

A Time to Question Everything

Now, how are you doing with that? How are you doing trusting that which you cannot see, which isn't visible to the naked eye, which eludes us at times because faith in God beckons us to reach out and take the hand of someone who left the earth two millennia ago? This doesn't make faith less real, it simply makes it more difficult, more challenging, more countercultural, and less normal. This also means that real faith in Jesus must be learned because it doesn't come easily.

Learning Faith in College

Scores of students major in religion, philosophy, biblical studies, or a host of other church-related words, but what happens if a student doesn't seek to simply obtain an academic degree; rather he or she seeks a personal experience of trusting Jesus? Can you imagine the conversation with their parents?

"So how is college going? How are your studies coming along?" asks a dad who is secretly pleased that so far he has paid for his daughter's private, Christian high school education and now is quietly proud of her excellent grades at a top-rated Christian college.

"I don't know," she responds.

"What do you mean?" he says.

"I mean, I like the classes and stuff, but I was really convicted in chapel the other day that maybe I should spend more time seeking to trust Jesus rather than just talking about him or reading other people's thoughts about him. So I am thinking about reducing my credits next semester to create space for this," says the young woman, who is owning her faith.

The dad's smile vanishes from his face. He is spending tens of thousands of dollars in tuition and this won't change during his daughter's experiment in faith. She may not graduate in four years and she may be destroying her resume. After all, how can she explain this to a future employer? "Let's be practical," is the only phrase streaming through his mind. The daughter studies her father's face and, for the first time, she knows that faith costs something.

Does this scenario resonate with you? Studies abound today about young people losing their faith in college, but are we truly prepared for students who have found their faith? I am not sure that we want students to either lose it or find it. I think that most parents are content to simply have their children grow into nice, moral people who mimic the Christian subculture's status quo. If this sounds harsh, think about it a bit more.

If you're a student, would your parent support you taking a semester off to serve the poor overseas or do a fellowship at a local church? If you're a parent, how would you react if your son or daughter stopped going to your church in favor of another church? What will we do with each other's doubt? What can we do with each other's faith? What is it that you and I truly believe?

My senior year in college, I was asked to speak at the on-campus worship service as one of several students reflecting on faith and their future. Of course, there were pep talks from faculty full of hope and there were a couple students who sang so well they could be recording artists. Then, there was me. I spoke from the text, "who do you say I am?" (Luke 9:20), which is often called Peter's confession of Christ, but in my remarks I never got much beyond the question. I did manage to say, "whoever we say Christ is will shape the rest of our lives in meaningful ways," but outside of that, I don't recall saying anything particularly moving or memorable. When the service ended, my plan to fade away into the lazy Sunday afternoon was interrupted by the president of the college shaking my hand. He commended me for asking such good questions and then he commended me for not having all the answers. I thanked him but still remember his words nearly twenty years later because I still ask questions and I still don't have all the answers. But now that I am older, fewer people are commending me for my continued desire to learn to live by faith.

By the time you are an adult, you are supposed to have fallen in line with something. Have you noticed that? If you are married, then people wonder when you are going to have kids, but if you're

A Time to Question Everything

not married, why not? When will you buy a house? Is this just a job or a career? The list goes on and on.

Then Jesus comes along, while you're tending to the myriad expectations from other people, and says, "but you, who do you say I am?" And your answer will disrupt all the other answers you give to all the questions coming at you from all the other people in your life. I learned at least this much about faith in college.

Learning Faith in Community

After college, the expectation is that you get a job or, if you go to graduate school, then the expectation rises and you better have a really good job. And this job is where you'll spend about 40 percent of your waking hours. So yes, your work is important as it will shape you in some way simply because it's where you spend the majority of your time. Work, though, isn't the first thing that shapes us. People shape us, relationships shape us, and this starts from day one.

Within a community, whether it's the family or workplace or athletic team or church, we tend to trust people before we trust God. Again, just pause and think about it. We cry for human attention because humans are the first thing that looks back at us or at least that's what we see. At some point we are taught that God too looks at us and has done so since before we even opened our eyes. In a world of chance and atheism, everyone enters the world alone, but in a world where God watches over all things, suddenly the baby that gets pushed down the river in a little basket, toward an Egyptian ruler, can be an instrument of deliverance for a race that has been enslaved for decades. Eventually, the baby boy is picked up and cared for in the house of the oppressor and only God knows that this little boy will grow up to be the Moses that other little children will read about several thousand years later. In fact, many of us first learned about Moses from other people and so the story survives thousands of years later to be shared in community, person to person. And it's through these two ways of learning that we first begin to trust God.

Faith Isn't Normal, is It?

We learn to trust God through watching other people. Before we understood what our parents said to us, we watched them. I have seen pictures of myself as a child dressing up like Batman and to this day, my mother loves to tell stories about when I would watch cartoons and within seconds of the show ending, I would be imitating what I saw. The same is true of the adults in my life. Before I knew how to talk, I could watch, learn, imitate, and observe other people. We often skip over this aspect of learning faith too quickly. Thomas à Kempis, in his classic work *The Imitation of Christ*, challenges us further with these words:

> You will find, apart from Him, that nearly all the trust you place in men is a total loss.. . ..You will quickly be deceived if you look only to the outward appearance of men, and you will often be disappointed if you seek comfort and gain in them. If, however, you seek Jesus in all things, you will surely find Him.[1]

As a child, though, we don't seek Jesus unless we see other people seeking Jesus. And herein lies one of the ongoing challenges to the church as well as to you and to me. It is true that God isn't finished with us yet, but let's be honest, we're not finished with each other yet either. We still watch, listen, and imitate people to see not only if their faith is real, but also to test our own faith. Can I live this faith out in real life? We don't think about this, really, until we've been watching people for years. This is not a negative thing. This is simply the way we often live and faith is initially learned through our immediate relationships.

In a way, I am reiterating a cliché that states, "faith is better caught than taught," but let me qualify the statement and rephrase it. I believe "faith is always caught and always taught" and the two are inseparable. So yes, faith is tested in relationships, but faith is also taught in relationships and the basic communication tool is that of telling stories. Remember those stories that shaped you as a child? You trusted both those stories and those storytellers, didn't you?

---

1. Kempis, *Imitation of Christ*, 42.

A Time to Question Everything

The vast majority of children learn about Abraham, Moses, Adam and Eve, David and Goliath, Daniel in the lion's den, and the fiery furnace, and the list of characters from stories that have been passed down from one generation to the next goes on. These stories are reminding us of God's grace and shaping us through our own imagination. Don't miss this. I believe the first two things that happen when we begin to exercise true faith is that our immediate relationships are tested and we begin to form an understanding of the world through the stories we are told. This incredible cycle begins as we hear stories told to us. We in turn tell these same stories to our closest friends and family, and suddenly, our stories not only are being told, but tested and, over time, this incredible exchange shapes who we are and how we live.

The people we trust will one day be tested by the stories we believe and this exchange shapes us and molds us, often in ways we don't understand until the gift of hindsight is given to us. Let's go a little deeper. If you are going to exercise true faith, you will begin doing so by exercising your imagination. Faith is a story of what we trust and what we deem reliable. I believe this is why we're so impacted by movies, music, and art. These expressive forms of communication help us engage with ideas on a new level that often gives us permission to look at things from another angle. True faith engages us deeply and asks us to consider a new way of life. This new way of life involves two fundamental changes. First, we must treat people differently, and second, we must often refine our understanding of the grander story that governs our decisions, ethics, and behavior. To trust Jesus more than other people requires not only that we seek to follow his teaching and understand his parables, but that we also begin to see other people in their proper place, not as less than human, but as less than God. In relationship with other people, we learn that we must serve and love one another if we truly trust Christ and truly want to usher in a new way of life that runs contrary to the onslaught of the me-first messages thrown at us in advertisements and social media. But we also learn faith through other people, because we recognize that flawed people hurt us, let us down, and fail us, and this drives us

Faith Isn't Normal, is It?

(hopefully) to keep seeking that one person, that one relationship, that will always be for our good, inviting us not to self-exaltation, but to self-sacrifice. So we listen to the stories around us and the stories we tell, and then we pay attention to the relationships we're building and the people we observe. At the intersection of story and relationship is where faith takes root and begins to flourish.

Learning Faith in Christ

When our faith matures through the intersection of story and relationship, the most visible fruit is love. But love isn't grown artificially so. In searching for a Christian life, one must engage with Christ himself. While our culture wants to learn faith in church or in college, if we're honest with ourselves, we all learn to trust someone or something through experience with that person or thing.

Let's take the example of hiring a babysitter. How do you decide if that person is going to be trustworthy enough to be with your own children or children you love while you're away? I am guessing that you will have had some previous contact with the babysitter. You may know his or her parents and you'll have seen them interact with other children, whether it's in church, school, or with another family. Then the fateful night comes when you give final instructions, post emergency numbers by the phone, and kiss the kids goodnight about seventy times prior to getting in the car for your date. The initial panic sets in and the entire ride to the restaurant is occupied by conversation about the kids. At some point, parents risk something and leave the children in the hands of the babysitter.

Now, let me challenge us both. When's the last time either of us truly risked taking Jesus at his word and left him in charge of our lives? No, this isn't normal, but neither is the Christian life. People who risk following Jesus must risk the American dream for sacrifice and service. People who risk following Jesus must risk loving people who have been left out and who are sometimes in left field. Think about it. Are there a lot of people in your workplace or in your neighborhood who refrain from gossip, love their enemies, care for widows and orphans, and turn the other cheek? These people would likely stick out precisely because welcoming strangers in and sacrificial giving aren't normal. People who spend any time at all truly trying to follow Jesus understand this rather quickly.

Learning Something Great is Hard

Many writers and motivational speakers have alluded to the endurance of Abraham Lincoln who seemed to lose political contests regularly before becoming one of the great leaders in U.S. history. William Wilberforce is also lauded for his endurance as he fought to end the slave trade, living with regular parliamentary defeat. Martin Luther King, Jr. was jailed for standing up for civil rights, and the list grows as we see that major movements in history involve great endurance. In our instant culture, this challenges us to think out farther, dig deeper, and settle in a bit because this is going to take some time.

If you ever took an easy class in college or felt cheated at times because something was a no-brainer and took no effort at all, then be encouraged, faith is the direct opposite. It's hard. It's difficult to stand up to the nonsense that the world says is success, and the pain that we cause others as well as the pain we endure from others. And positive thinking isn't enough. Sometimes people hurt us deeply and sometimes close friends and family members die. Then what? Is your answer to the pain and evil in this world going to truly be "well, let's just look at the bright side?"

No, you are intellectually and spiritually smarter than that. We all are smarter than that, so we all must find something that we can lean on, something that holds our whole weight, something that keeps our pride in check when we're successful, and something that keeps our world from crashing down when we fail. Let me pause a moment and make an important distinction. Faith isn't the same as fanaticism, nor is it the absence of all doubt. Faith in the finished work of Christ avoids both relativism on the one hand (anything goes, truth isn't absolute) and fundamentalism

Faith Isn't Normal, is It?

on the other hand (we have superior insight into truth, everyone else has nothing good to contribute). Faith admits our need for a Savior, but simultaneously confesses our dignity as human beings and holds these two truths perfectly in tension so that we know we are created as unique, reasonable, and precious persons in the image of God. We also know with great clarity that we are flawed, imperfect, and are in need of mercy and grace.

In the United States, we're taught over and again that certainty is somehow bad, but this is simply a position that cannot be lived out culturally. At some point, we still rely on (trust, if you will) our institutions to provide certain boundaries and freedoms. We are certain that a red light means stop and we are certain that our drinking water should be safe and that our sewage systems should work and that "anything goes" certainly doesn't apply to homeland security or our neighbor's daily whims and emotions. Peter Berger writes, "While a doubter can carefully consider the facts, the possibilities, and the options available, eventually choices have to be made and actions taken."[2] So doubt has its place, but it also has its limits. We know this all too well and, if we're honest, we understand clearly that we truly lean on someone or something daily to both comfort and guide us. Whether it's our own intellect, our own abilities, our friends, our Bill of Rights, or the person and work of Christ, we put our weight on someone or something and believe that such trust will come through for us.

But in the end, only Jesus endures the ups and downs of our life. Think about it. If you trust your intellect, what will you do when you're wrong? If you trust your own abilities, well, what can you do when faced with something bigger than you? Our friends and family will let us down at some point, and the list grows. So we move away from what is normal and commonplace toward that which is greater and more satisfying. Jesus invites us to experience something that will satisfy our intellectual, emotional, spiritual, moral, and existential needs. Sure, it's difficult to leave every other thing behind to lean on Jesus, but that's also part of the invitation. Try leaning on your own ability and your own intellect and

---

2. Berger and Zijderveld, *In Praise of Doubt*, 122.

A Time to Question Everything

try putting your whole trust in other people and eventually these normal modes of seeking peace of conscience, peace in the world, and peace in your deepest soul will leave you parched or disappointed (and potentially depressed or cynical). The Christian life is difficult, but so is everything else that means a great deal to us.

Learning from Great Guides

Up to this point, I have wanted to point out in personal and illustrative ways the fact that we all must deal with our wants and desires as we strive to live a Christian life. And within these wants and desires, we must come to grips with our own impatience, anxiety, and limitations if we are to truly find rest and joy by grace through faith. I will submit to you that an enduring Christian life is one that goes deeper and deeper until our great hungers are met, satisfied with what God gives to us in Christ Jesus. This process of becoming satisfied with what Jesus has done and will do in us and in this world is messy and involves all sorts of ups and downs; good days and awful days. We will, then, get lost every so often and will need divine guidance and human guides as well. These guides may come in the form of mentors you can have coffee with or they may be books you can read, underline, and highlight. We need our boredom interrupted and our wisdom challenged. We need to learn how to love. Good guides do this on the good days and on the bad days.

When Bad News and Bad Moods Come

At some point, we will not only struggle with our own meager faith in God, but we will receive bad news. How we respond will reveal the progress we have made thus far. We will also all face those days where we are greatly tempted due to being in a poor mood, downcast, or dejected.

At some point, we will all come face to face with this reality: we sometimes don't feel like following Jesus or exercising our

Faith Isn't Normal, is It?

faith. We simply want to do what feels good, and often this leads to impulsive and destructive actions because unless we filter our emotions through the grid of grace, we will live in our default mode of self-preservation that quickly leads to self-exaltation. Let me encourage you (and me for that matter) to fight the bad days and bad moods with what you know is most trustworthy—namely trusting in Christ, who alone beckons us to believe that all things are being made new.

Remember the Gift of Faith

One of the more helpful books on introducing Christian doctrine I have found is *Concise Theology* by J. I. Packer. Curiously, there is no chapter devoted to the topic of faith alone. Instead, faith is described in three other chapters, namely ones referring to works, repentance, and regeneration. In other words, Packer reiterates in summary what we intuitively know, which is that faith is a gift and not something we can manufacture or squeeze out of the raw material we carry around. Packer describes it in these terms,

> The concept is of God renovating the heart, the core of a person's being, by implanting a new principle of desire, purpose, and action, a dispositional dynamic that finds expression in positive response to the gospel and its Christ.[3]

So you see the progression don't you? First, there is a heart change brought on by God, and second, there is a change of mind brought on by God, the fruit of which is faith or trust in God. Faith is a response to what God initiated. Sometimes, we act like faith is something we must muster up because things aren't going our way, but that's simply not the case. Faith is the way we live all of life because it is the fruit of having our heart and mind changed. You might say our wants and desires have been redeemed.

---

3. Packer, *Concise Theology*, 157.

A Time to Question Everything

When We Need God

In our culture of self-sufficiency with self-made millionaires or self-taught athletes and self-conscious celebrities, how do we remember that there is not one second of the day in which we don't need God? Since God is love, there is not a second of any day in which we don't need the sustaining import of giving and receiving love. Naturally, our loves are fickle and dependent on receiving the good will of another. We don't often see or experience what we say we believe. So we need love and, subsequently, since so much of what we see falls short, we need God. Eugene Peterson puts it this way: "A person has to be thoroughly disgusted with the way things are to set out on the Christian way."[4] Some people, though, will resist, deny, or do whatever they can to avoid feeling like there's a need for help. Certainly, seeking the help of God in a culture filled with technological advances and the promise of indefinite progress seems simple. Some cultural messages that are aimed at us though, are also lying to us.

The onslaught of messages that we receive and digest are all predicated on the idea that we can quite readily fix our own problems or that we're fine until further notice. And yet another idea is that we are to follow or imitate the example of Jesus. One may protest in this way: How can we try to imitate someone who doesn't live on earth? This is why being at least minimally interested in the words of Jesus and at best, captivated and caught up in his teachings, remains an important part of anyone interested in taking a stab at the Christian life. Again, Peterson is helpful when he writes,

> We are not scavenging in the dark alleys of the world, poking in its garbage cans for bare subsistence. We are traveling in the light, toward God who is rich in mercy and strong to save. It is Christ, not culture, that defines our lives. It is the help we experience, not the hazards we risk, that shapes our days.[5]

---

4. Peterson, *Long Obedience*, 25.
5. Ibid., 79.

Faith Isn't Normal, is It?

Remember: Don't Stop Halfway

Now we come back to the issue of learning faith in Christ and in this respect, we must say that truly learning something means truly giving oneself to the subject or the person without reservation. No one learns to ride a bicycle by keeping one foot constantly on the ground. At some point you need to peddle the bike with both feet. And similarly, no one learns to swim by sitting on the edge of the pool with dangling legs splashing in the water. At some point you need to have your whole body in the deep end of the pool. The same is true of faith in Jesus.

It's quite one thing to say that Christ is the antidote for your anxiety or your sorrow and Jesus helps you to hope in troubled times, thereby giving you more patience than you'd normally have, but this isn't the same as a wholly different life. J. I. Packer guides us in this direction:

> Why. . .do we appear as no more than halfway Christians? Whence comes the nervous, dithery, take-no-risks mood that mars so much of our discipleship? Why are we not free enough from fear and anxiety to allow ourselves to go full stretch in following Christ?[6]

Now these are questions we can return to often. What is stopping you or me or others from truly following hard after Jesus? Packer continues, "One reason, it seems, is that in our heart of hearts we are afraid of the consequences of going the whole way into the Christian life."[7] So, we dangle our feet on the side of it or we try to put one foot in several places so that we leave our proverbial options open, but we don't go all the way. Packer concludes,

> This, at bottom, seems to be what is wrong with us. We are afraid to go all the way in accepting the authority of God, because of our secret uncertainty as to his adequacy to look after us if we do. Now, let us call a spade a spade. The name of the game we are playing is unbelief. . . .[8]

6. Packer, *Knowing God*, 269.
7. Ibid., 269–79.
8. Ibid., 270.

A Time to Question Everything

The sobering reality is that the root cause of so many of our struggles in life is simply unbelief. We're afraid to lean our whole weight on the grace of God and we're afraid to bet the farm on the fact that God truly loves us and truly is restoring all things, making all things new, perfecting us in the image of Christ, and singing over us with delight. Why can't we accept what God says about us in Christ? Why must we continue to kick against his kindness, demanding our way, and reacting when we don't get what we want?

I can hear us all say, but how does one have the kind of faith that lets go of anxiety and helplessness? How can I have the faith to trust that God cares about me before I do good works, not after I do the work? How can I have the faith to understand that I have limitations and God does not?

Perhaps, though, these questions are poor ones. The phrase "how do I" places the emphasis again on what we can do or on our response. Perhaps the better way is to accept what has been done by God over what I may do today or tomorrow. What happens if I wake up tomorrow morning and truly live like I have been forgiven and set free from the tyranny of shame, selfishness, and sin? What does a person act like whose debt has been eternally paid and whose shame has been covered with love and grace? What happens if I simply grow up into a person who truly believes that death has no hold on me and that every person I meet is created in the image of God?

I believe two things would happen. First, we wouldn't ask how to do something, we would simply act and react out of who we are, who God has redeemed us to be. And second, we would find out rather quickly that truly accepting the reality of the grace of God would make us, well, not quite normal.

"I can't understand why you believe all this stuff, " says the skeptic who may be a voice in our head or a real person in front of us.

And then, to lean our whole weight on the grace of God, we will say something rather odd. We will respond in gentleness with grace and truth without a hint of anger or defensiveness and we will simply say, "I can't understand life any other way."

Faith Isn't Normal, is It?

"How can you say that?" scolds the skeptic. "Surely you can see alternatives in this world to your faith or your God. Surely you can concede that you may be wrong."

"But the alternatives leave grace out of the picture—they're all about trying harder, being better, picking yourself up off the floor," says the messed up believer.

After a long pause, we quietly add, "By the grace of God, I am what I am." Now back to your regularly-scheduled, normal life. That is, unless you're ready to move on to bigger and better things. The Christian life does get better, doesn't it?

12

Who Do You Trust?

"None of us knows what might happen even the next minute, yet still we go forward. Because we trust. Because we have Faith."

—Paulo Coehlo, *Brida*

THE GOD YOU'RE MOST interested in is the one you tend to follow. Think about it. If you're bored in church, your mind goes to other things and frankly, to other gods. This might be the idol of success or the tyranny of the clock, but at some point, with a Bible propped open on your lap and a hymnal sitting right in front of you, your mind goes to other things. Even more dramatic, praise songs projected on giant screens that cannot be missed, you become less interested in the person and work of Jesus and more interested in lesser things. And this is why all the other gods retain a bit of power.

Have you ever heard someone say something like this: "Why can't so-and-so be more tolerant?" Don't you sometimes want to raise your hand and ask, "Tolerant of what? Of whom? And when do we stop being tolerant, because it seems everyone has a line that cannot be crossed?"

Who Do You Trust?

So what is that line that cannot be crossed for you? That line, in my opinion, is what has captured your heart; that line is directly related to the god that most interests you—right now.

And right now is what you can truly impact. You cannot do a thing about yesterday and tomorrow is completely out of your control. The only moment in which you can truly make a difference is right now. Today, you can impact someone's life. Right now, you can trust another person. In this moment, you can hold another person's hand, feel the whisper of a lover on your ear, get chills at the touch of someone who is present with you. And whoever you trust is the one allowed to move closer, sit right next to you, and see what you see. The question is this: Who do you really trust?

Feel the Whisper

According to research, the human eardrum will split open at 150 decibels or above.[1] An airplane takes off at around ninety to one hundred decibels, and a human whisper, by contrast, comes in at twenty decibels. The softness of a whisper means that it's both quiet and close.

The one we trust the most is the one who shows us grace. The one who creates space for us to be imperfect versions of our best self is the one we allow close enough to feel their breath on our flesh. Think about that one person or those few people who can lean over and whisper in to your ear without creeping you out. Now that's a small and priceless circle, isn't it? Most of us will flinch when someone leans their head toward us (or scream, depending on the person), but to those who we lean toward to make it easier for the whisper to be heard, those are special people. Whether one of those is God or not, the reality is the same: we only listen to whispers from those we trust.

---

1. "Noise Sources and Their Effects."

A Time to Question Everything

Occupying Personal Space

Sometimes I get the middle seat on a plane and my personal space takes a beating. Oh, I don't get physically beat up, but complete strangers sit within inches of me. On international flights, he or she will toss and turn and do never-before-seen yoga positions to try to get some sleep. All the while, you're just sitting in the middle trying to get the movie controls to work and the headset properly adjusted. People you trust though can do almost anything they want without really bothering you, because you want them to occupy what is commonly called personal space.

If you're like me, then sometimes you'd like nothing better than to wake up with a trusted friend leaning on your shoulder. I could care less if someone I love props their feet on me, falls asleep on my arm, or sits closer because she is cold and that airline air conditioning is set at just above freezing. Those I trust can sit inside my own space because it's my space which they have so positively impacted already.

Sharing Bad News About . . . Me

We all know that the people we love know some things about us that others don't. We have memories created through shared life and we can remember that one song at the concert, that one dessert that we shoved down even though it was a dinosaur-size portion, and that one important city or landmark that only certain people get to see. Only the ones we really trust get the late-night phone call to receive bad news—about us. Only my inner circle gets the "I really screwed up," version of me.

And this is an integral part of trust. The general public can see the unvarnished version of me, that's the moments in life when I just don't care, but the typical person on the street won't get me to confess the bad stuff that I did. The bad news about me is one thing, but the bad news about me—from me—that's the game changer. And that's only for people I trust.

Who Do You Trust?

The answer to who we trust lies in the combination of who we'd share personal space with, who we don't mind whispering in our ear, and who loves us when we share bad news about ourselves. Over time, faith or this reliance becomes something magical, mystical, and so life-giving that we'd do one more thing that demonstrates trust. We'd defend them no matter what.

Fighting for Others

This is the mystery of the gospel of grace and the amazing part of trust. Once we share the bad news about ourselves, the ones we trust do something that defies conventional logic. They turn against the world and defend us. Okay, maybe that's a little dramatic, but nonetheless, it always feels liberating and loving as we see our name defended despite the fact that we know we have blown it at times. This cements the trust. This seals the proverbial deal. This is what we long for and we will fight for those who do this for us. Go ahead and count how many "friends" on Facebook will defend you and fight for you. That's a very different number than the "friend" number isn't it? There are, of course, other experiences we've had with people.

I have felt discarded by friends and likely some friends have felt ignored by me. Neither action engendered trust. On the contrary, trust diminishes like a fading candle wick. Yet, one of the least-known benefits of growing up in a small town (in my case, less than 5,000 people) is that some friends last a lifetime and some people still think nice things because you'll always be one of them. There is a shared identity when we fight for others, and something remarkable happens when we defend another person: we actually grow in our love for them. Amazing grace leads to increased love which leads to growing trust. Will we get hurt in the process? Yes. But that's part of the deal and that's how you know you've actually put yourself out there and on the line for someone else. If it doesn't hurt, you may not be risking much. Trust or, dare I call it, faith is inseparably linked to risk.

A Time to Question Everything

Here's the truth: You and I can afford to risk a little more in loving people today than we did yesterday.

The link between risk and faith or risk and trust should not be taken lightly. We are way too quick to think our brilliance is the reason for knowing who we should hang with or who we should avoid. Wise men and women, though, still get hurt in this world. Ken Gire reminds us that pain can lead us to something better. He writes,

> From my own tears I have learned that if you follow your tears, you will find your heart. If you find your heart, you will find what is dear to God. And if you find what is dear to God, you will find the answer to how you should live your life.[2]

Tears, though, are part of being vulnerable. Vulnerability leaves us in the humbling position of potentially being let down, and yet we trust anyway, we love anyway. There is no other way in which we can be fully present to one another, to God, to our lover, to a friend, unless we are willing to risk something—and stick it out for a long time. There is no escape clause when it comes to love and grace. In fact, the very absence of escape makes us love more and extend grace more. When we're not looking for ways out of relationships, love and grace will find their way in to the relationship.

This is how change begins to work its way out into the neighborhood. We can be catalysts who change one authentic relationship at a time.

---

2. Gire, *Windows of the Soul*, 195.

13

Is Grace Strong Enough for this World?

"Why grace? Because some days, it's the only thing we have in common. Because it's the one thing I'm certain is real. Because it's the reason I'm here."

—Cathleen Falsani, *Sin Boldly*

THE GREATEST WAY WE can fight terrorism, poverty, disease, and dysfunction is found in extending a fierce grace that is grounded in sacrificial love.

Grace is not a masculine word, but it's a tough word. Grace has a soft sound, but a hard edge. Can grace take on the viral videos of beheadings or the fervent fear of ebola outbreaks? The answer is yes.

Grace is not just our last hope against the darkness inside us, but it's the only hope for the darkness outside us.

Remember the daydream of me sitting in church with a cigarette and subsequently getting kicked out? Like cigarettes in church, toxic words and negativity seem out of place with grace.

A Time to Question Everything

Yet, we inhale a lot of hateful rhetoric and we digest too much discord through our media. It's hard to take it all in, especially in large doses. Why can't there be a place where people could inhale grace? Warning labels abound against nicotine, spelling out the dangers of toxins and the perils of secondhand smoke, but where are the labels that warn against cynicism and putting so much negativity into our bloodstream that toxic apathy or secondhand disappointment spills out? Grace changes everything, but it needs to be internalized daily.

While working with international crisis response at the University of Illinois in the summer of 2014, I responded to a missing persons case involving a student who had disappeared off the Brazilian coastline. A friend who spoke Portuguese translated for me over the phone as we talked to the rescue operations commander daily. I still remember making the phone call to the parents with the news that their son will probably never be found. To this day, there isn't much closure. And yes, this is part of the world we live in. These things happen to people and we want an explanation that will satisfy the pain, the cry, and the devastating loss. Sometimes, though, words fail us and there are no good explanations.

And so we work harder, try harder, think harder about how things like this will never happen again. But they do. Earthquakes devastate cities and buildings topple onto parents and children. Tornadoes rip through towns and pictures of shredded homes haunt our television. The world we live in can be a difficult, cruel place at times. Yet grace is tougher than whatever the world can throw at us. This toughness causes us to question everything else because every single day, we're reminded by both the wicked and the good, the kind and the cruel, that what matters most is that people get what they deserve. We want our rights to be satisfied and so grace is considered a bit weaker than bold-sounding words like "injustice" and "outcry." Yet returning love instead of hate, unmerited favor instead of earned status, changes everything, and this is especially true if grace can be shown every day over a long period of time. Grace strengthens communities and relationships,

Is Grace Strong Enough for this World?

and because of its power it strengthens the entire world. In fact, grace is the only thing strong enough to *take on* the entire world.

Inseparable: Grace and Truth

Grace, though, isn't single. She's eternally married to truth and they always show up together. This is what makes grace so strong. She's never alone. Truth makes us see reality for what it is while grace moves us to care deeply, move closer, and reach out a compassionate hand. In fact, until truth is truly embraced, grace is almost impossible to extend or even experience. Grace and truth are inseparable.

Randy Alcorn is helpful when he writes that

> Truth without grace is unbending, like the law of gravity. Gravity doesn't take into consideration the fact that the individual in the car is young, kind, tired, or didn't mean to get too close to the edge of the cliff. When the car plunges off the precipice, gravity shows no sympathy. Truth tells us we're sick. Only grace can cure us.[1]

Grace and truth together allow us to confront a confusing, broken world as well as the confusing and broken person looking at us every morning in the mirror. Alcorn concludes:

> Isn't it patronizing to withhold truth from people because we imagine they can't handle it? Grace always deals with truth, and offers forgiveness when there's been wrongdoing. The way to no longer feel guilty is not to deny guilt, but to face it and ask God's forgiveness. Grace liberates us.[2]

An often-quoted text in the world of ideas and even at universities is that "the truth will set you free" (John 8: 31–32). Again, only truth, inseparably linked to grace, sets us free. Truth with no grace beats us down. Grace with no truth is like a fairy tale, minimizing reality. Grace and truth together can liberate an entire

1. Alcorn, "Grace and Truth Paradox," paras. 106—7.
2. Ibid., para. 157.

community and together are strong enough to take on this violent world.

Instructive: Grace Can Say No

Grace doesn't always say yes. Isn't that a bit shocking? We typically think of grace as that which always makes something more tolerable or easier to swallow. Grace, to some people, is warm and fuzzy all the time. Some people confuse grace with permission or permissiveness.

"If you try to follow the teachings of Jesus, you'll limit your fun," said the tempter. And then the serpent whispers to all of us at one time or another, "Did God really say that the gospel is good news?"

In Titus 2:12, we read some rather remarkable words that often get skipped over. They are as follows: "For the grace of God has appeared that offers salvation for all people. It teaches us to say 'No' to ungodliness and worldly passions, and to live self-controlled, upright, and godly lives in this present age" (NIV).

The reason for waiting or for saying no is found in verse 13, which is equally remarkable: "while we wait for the blessed hope—the appearing of the glory of our great God and Savior Jesus Christ, who gave himself up to redeem us from all wickedness and to purify for himself a people that are his very own, eager to do good" (NIV).

Grace teaches us to say no in the short term to things that are *not good* because we are anticipating the fulfillment of what we hope for, namely the return of Jesus, who will reconnect with his own people who are characterized by an eagerness "to do good." If you have truly experienced grace, then you have truly screwed something up. My guess is that somewhere along the way, you grew tired of waiting and your impatience led to something less than good. In fact, impatience has been fundamental to virtually every bad decision I have ever made. I think this is why 1 Corinthians 13 says that "love is patient." Impatience is neither loving nor gracious. Grace, though, teaches us to say yes to patient love and no to self-absorbed hurry. Take a deep breath and think about that for a moment. Grace allows us to slow down and recalibrate in an eagerness to do the right thing.

Intolerable: The Company Grace Keeps

Would you say that any of your friends are sinners? It's not really an en vogue term nor is it flattering to say the least. The company grace keeps, though, is often intolerable to the status quo. Church-going people even muttered, "why does Jesus eat with sinners and tax collectors?" (Luke 5:27–32). The life of Jesus became intolerable for a variety of reasons, but one of them is most certainly because grace invites everyone to the table and we aren't accustomed to the rich, the poor, the powerful, the weak, Sunday school teachers, and unbelieving drug addicts all dining at the same table. And the list grows from there. Grace is strong enough to build a table big enough for every person who has ever blown it.

Yet I think we still give ourselves a bit of a pass on this one. We will keep colorful company as long as we are not identified publicly with that company or stained by his or her reputation. After all, once someone is known for screwing up, few people are quick to point to them and say "That messed up person. Yeah, that one. That's my friend," and this makes grace almost intolerable to so many people. It seems cheap because messed up people get the benefits that they don't deserve. And that's exactly the point. Grace, by its very definition, cannot be deserved or earned. The company grace keeps is controversial because we want to distance ourselves from those who don't perform well, who don't love well, who don't smell good, or who don't make us look better. Yet a true experience of grace will drive us toward all people who are in need and that introduces us to a messy world indeed.

A Time to Question Everything

Inspirational: Grace is Unique

Only Jesus, only Christianity, emphasizes a message of grace; all other worldviews prioritize performance or pragmatism. The American Dream is not a message of grace. It's a message of picking oneself up from low positions and it's often interpreted as a self-made story. Grace inspires us because there is nothing like it anywhere else on planet earth.

And this is why so many people settle for "how-to" books and information that sets us up as the ones who earn their rewards. Yet grace is harder, more work, and it's life-changing stuff. Grace makes room for dialogue with other faiths without giving in to the temptation to prove ourselves or defend our good work. Grace tells us it's okay to listen, to learn, and to live freely in this complex world. The scandalous part of grace is that if you follow the noble path in Buddhism or stay rigorously disciplined in Islam or patiently wait in Judaism or commit spiritually to any other organized worldview, the result is the same. Only grace closes the gaps between everything that is broken. Whether it's you and creation, you and God, you and your neighbors, or you and your own inner demons, all that is broken can be put back together. If there was a periodic table for worldviews, grace would be the rarest element in the world. Philip Yancey is right in saying that "Only Christianity dares to make God's love unconditional."[3] Our acceptance comes before our response. And this is grace. Paul Zahl adds, "The law, the stress of life driving you to a breakdown, reduces you to a walking question mark. The question is answered, amazingly, by God's one-way love. Grace changes everything."[4]

So the strength of grace comes because it's truly instructive to us, inseparably linked to truth, intolerable in its willingness to identify with imperfect people, and inspirational in its allure and uniqueness. Grace is why it's okay to invite someone else to consider walking alongside you in this journey and grace is why the twists and turns of life are worth the experience. Whatever tries to

---

3. Yancey, *What's so Amazing about Grace?*, 11.
4. Zahl, *Grace in Practice*, 91.

Is Grace Strong Enough for this World?

knock you down, try fighting differently. What would it look like to retaliate regularly and over time with grace? If we extend grace long enough, we'll start to gain momentum and strength and will likely hear something to the effect of "hey, we didn't see that coming," and to everyone's surprise, things will never be the same. And don't you think that sometimes, different is a good thing?

14

Is This Worth the Trip?

> "Not all those who wander are lost."
> —J. R. R. Tolkien, *The Fellowship of the Ring*

> "Our heavenly Father won't give up until each one of his children has completed the journey."
> —Paul David Tripp, *A Quest for Something More*

"Do you know how fast you were going?" asked the police officer. All of my belongings were crammed in my trunk the backseat and sprawled on the passenger seat as I drove from Iowa to St. Louis.

"No sir," I replied.

The police officer took several moments to look at the mess in my car.

"Where are you going with all of this?" he asked.

"I am heading to seminary," I replied.

A smile came over the trooper's face.

Is This Worth the Trip?

"I haven't heard that one yet and I have heard a lot of things," he said through a smile.

I said nothing, too nervous to be creative and embarrassed that I had already blurted out something rather awkward.

"Consider this a warning and slow down, okay?" he said.

I nodded.

He tapped the roof of my car and then tapped the trunk again. I can see the smile still on his face as he waved me on—my signal to go ahead and keep driving. I was on my way to start seriously studying the Bible and I already had been pulled over by the long arm of the law. I shook my head and thought to myself, "God, I am not sure about this."

Have you ever felt a bit out of place, but knew you were in the right place anyway? While everyone I met in seminary was broken, some seemed to act like they belonged in a pulpit. I just wanted to belong to God. In a very real way, I think I was looking for some kind of home. I wanted a place that was both life-affirming and life-giving as well. I wanted to find me and find others and that's no small task.

By God's mercy, grace met me in that place and I saw professors truly living what they were teaching and I saw classmates truly seeking answers to deep questions. Those years were incredibly influential; those years, though, are not where the journey ends.

One Step at a Time

A few years back, while in the belly of a depression, I visited a psychologist I liked who referred me to a psychiatrist that I did not like at all. I have benefited greatly from counselors and pastors over the years, but I have struggled with others. Whether it was a scheduling issue or some miscommunication, I sat across from a rude man who, for at least a month, told me that I was emotionally repressed and out of touch with myself. During our last session, I heard these words: "You're so emotionally repressed. I know Jesus. I know spirituality better than you do."

A Time to Question Everything

Alone and dejected after these meetings, I tried to journal and write to make sense of why God had me trying to battle depression with difficult people. The right people and the right words at the right time are sometimes elusive. The rights words, though, often come in the context of relationships. For the record, I did find a great counselor who agreed that I was a bit of a mess. This same counselor said that he'd like to help me understand my story better. He allowed me to embrace both the good news of grace and the bad days that are part of a very human story.

Yet sometimes I am afraid. I live with an undercurrent of melancholy and sometimes I can't help it. I know the well-meaning, clichéd answers that are supposed to be battle-tested and true, but that's not how my life works. We are all a cocktail of intellectual progress, spiritual convictions, and emotional need.

I need a deep faith because my great need is below the surface.

And so I come back to a blank sheet of paper and wonder how to respond to the prompting of God. I wish an angel would sit down in this Starbucks and tell me that things will turn out fine and that the plan laid out for me will get easier, but that's not happening. In fact, as I journal, I start to imagine myself conversing with an angel who will look out for me. Sometimes, imagining a conversation helps guide my thoughts and, if you're like me, the story we tell ourselves is extremely important. After all, we're going to believe what we preach to ourselves, what we rehearse in our minds, and what we repeat to our conscience.

"So, how does that make you feel? When the world seems to kick you while you're down, how do you respond?" asks an unnamed angel who may be my guardian. Gabriel and Michael always seem to get the bigger projects and I am not in that category yet.

"I want to beat that man in the face," I reply. The angel nods hesitantly.

"Maybe you do have emotional problems," says the angel who breaks the uncomfortable silence.

Is This Worth the Trip?

I don't tell the angel off, but he knows (or she, I can't tell, too much heavenly light, exaggerated glow, you know, it's a fricking angel) I am upset.

"You were about to say something," the angel says.

I nod.

"Are you okay?" the angel asks.

"I am afraid."

The angel sits back and seems to relax a bit. A half smile appears and then the angel speaks.

"I have heard that one before, you know."

I nod.

"Can I tell you something?" asks the angel.

I nod.

"Grace isn't a 'get out of jail free' card. Grace means you'll never be in jail alone."

This time I neither nod nor shake my head. I just look at the angel.

"Do you understand? God will never, ever, leave you or forsake you."

I can feel the tears coming up again from some deep, dark, hidden place. You know, it's that secret entry in your journal that you want to keep locked away. It's that dark memory you visit unexpectedly. The tears are coming from that kind of place.

"God will never forsake you."

The voices, though, in this world. . .what about the encouragement to be better, try harder, or do this or that more? I know other people see me through the lens of this world. I have heard people tell me that I am no good or that I don't fit in or that I am one of those sinners. Sometimes friends don't call back and, hell, I live in a world that invented the word "unfriend." We unfriend each other all the time and call it social media. How screwed up is that? Yet this doesn't get said out loud because the angel's voice is getting louder and more powerful.

"God will never leave you or forsake you. God will never leave you or forsake you."

A Time to Question Everything

I am going to let God down again, I am going to do something stupid. I don't want to, but. . ."

"God will never forsake you."

Now, the tears drip out of my eyes like rain falling down a clear window.

The angel leans forward and draws uncomfortably close, but by this time, I can't see through my own glassy eyes. And then the angel whispers in to my ear.

"You will dwell in the house of the Lord forever. . .."

Silence.

Awe.

Prayer.

Lord have mercy.

Deep breath.

Squeeze eyes shut.

Open to a new normal.

Over fifteen years have passed since I put myself in the emergency room with well-meaning doctors trying to ascertain if I wanted to kill myself or not. I still battle depression at times and I find that the path that leads to peace is traveled one step at a time. I have not met a real angel—that I know of—but I believe God has sent messengers to interrupt both dysfunctional days and my cluttered mind. I believe in using my imagination when I journal and I believe that God meets me as much in the dark as he does in the light of day. I am learning that God is truly with us and sometimes he sends men and women into the path we're walking so that we can wake up and smell what Eden used to be.

When I was a young boy, I wanted to play professional baseball. One of the beauties of baseball is that it's a game that you cannot hurry. There is no shot clock, no two-minute warning, and no intermission. Baseball is a game where you must play your position indefinitely and without looking at the clock. In other words, you need to stay awake because at any moment, the ball may suddenly come screaming at you. Baseball also has the incredible tension of individual moments within the context of a team sport. Every player is spread out enough on the field and every player will eventually try to hit the ball, so at some point in the game, each player will be on their own. And yet at no point in the game is a player on his or her own. Each player is part of a team.

As you travel through this life, you will be faced with decisions that only you can make, and yet you will never be alone when you make them. You will have to make choices that only you can make, and yet people will be impacted by your choices. So our journeys will continue one step at a time, in the tension of our wants and desires, and we will be faced with daily temptations to look for cleaner, more comfortable roads to walk. Our wants and desires, though, will never be satisfied with the clean and the comfortable because life so often takes unexpected twists and turns, and frankly, none of us know what's coming tomorrow or the next day. Jack Miller writes that "we believe Jesus came in to the world to bring people a new life,"[1] and this new life is one giant sacred mess this side of heaven. Let me be clear. God isn't finished with us yet. Eric Alexander, a Scottish preacher and author, reminds us that "Whatever we need throughout our Christian pilgrimage, we have a guarantee in God's incomparable grace that he will supply it."[2] The incomparable grace expressed in this thing we call the Christian faith may be the only hope for what ails you, me, and this bittersweet world. In fact, this grace is both the fuel for the journey and the reward. And if you've truly experienced authentic grace, then you know it's worth every single mile of the journey. Malcolm Muggeridge once wrote, "The essential feature, and necessity of life is to know reality, which means knowing God. Otherwise our mortal existence is, as Saint Teresa of Avila said, no more than a night in a second-class hotel."[3] Let me just add that grace makes reality something we can swallow without choking on the cynicism or negativity that often pollutes the air. Outside "a second class

---

1. Miller, *Faith Worth Sharing*, 111.
2. Alexander, *Our Great God and Saviour*, 62.
3. Muggeridge, "Great Liberal Death Wish," para. 24.

A Time to Question Everything

hotel," there's great beauty and promise and hope because we're rebuilding, by grace, something new through creative compassion and redeeming love. This can get difficult, but it's worth the trip.

Fleming Rutledge states it this way: "Because he has rewritten the story, we do not have to be prisoners of our worst selves anymore."[4] We can love generously and we can give sacrificially. The world doesn't need our critical spirit or our cynical attitude. The world needs us to extend grace because you and I experience grace every day. A new day isn't given to every person in this world. And while this may seem like a heavy idea, grace holds the weight of all the things that may drag us down.

Grace is a weighty matter because it shows up when there's darkness or desperation. Grace is what we remember on our good days and what we need on our bad days. Grace is the best part of our story and grace shows us up when we are at our worst. Grace is accused of being cheap, because it's simultaneously incredibly valuable and free. And we don't know how to treat the free offer of anything very well. All of us want to take credit for our success or blame someone else when things go wrong. Grace will let us fall down because grace is masterful at picking us up. Can you put the weight of your life on the strength of God's grace? This is the question that reframes all other questions.

This is the invitation to something new.

If you're interested, don't feel like you need to take this journey alone. If you ever need someone to walk with you, let me know; we'll press on side by side. Pilgrims like us need to stick together. The road ahead will test us and sometimes we'll fall. Sometimes we'll trip on our own two feet and sometimes we will get blindsided by life itself. When we do, let's commit to picking one another back up off the ground and walking on.

We press on toward something better.

And we can all start again, do everything over, reboot our entire system. We can give more, love more, spread more kindness, and generously hand out grace.

Someone we walk by today will need grace.

---

4. Rutledge, *Help My Unbelief*, 108.

Is This Worth the Trip?

Someone we work with, live with, and lead will need grace. Someone needs your generous, unconditional love today. And someday, that person in need may just be you or me.

Bibliography

Alcorn, Randy. "The Grace and Truth Paradox: Excerpts." http://www.epm.org/resources/2010/Mar/23/grace-and-truth-paradox-excerpts/.
Alexander, Eric. *Our Great God and Saviour*. Edinburgh: Banner of Truth Trust, 2010.
Allender, Dan, and Tremper Longman. *Bold Love*. Colorado Springs, CO: NavPress, 1992.
Barrs, Jerram. *Echoes of Eden*. Wheaton, IL: Crossway, 2013.
Berger, Peter L., Anton Zijderveld. *In Praise of Doubt*. New York: HarperOne, 2009.
The Book of Common Prayer. New York: Church Publishing Inc., 2007. https://www.episcopalchurch.org/files/book_of_common_prayer.pdf.
Brown, Deneen L. "Martin Luther King's Scorn for the White Moderate." *Washington Post*, January 15, 2018. https://www.washingtonpost.com/news/retropolis/wp/2018/01/15/martin-luther-king-jr-s-scathing-critique-of-white-moderates-from-the-birmingham-jail/?utm_term=.c31a665ec984.
Brown, Steve. *Scandalous Freedom*. Brentwood, TN: Howard, 2004.
Chesterton, G. K. *What's Wrong with the World?* San Francisco: Ignatius, 1994.
Crabb, Larry. *The Pressure's Off*. Colorado Springs, CO: Waterbrook, 2002.
Crouch, Andy. *Culture Making*. Downers Grove, IL: InterVarsity, 2009.
Dostoyevsky, Fyodor. *The Gospel in Dostoyevsky*. Edited by The Bruderhof. Farmington, PA: Plough Publishing House of The Bruderhof Foundation, 1998.
Emba, Christine. "What is White Privilege?" *Washington Post*, January 16, 2016. https://www.washingtonpost.com/blogs/post-partisan/wp/2016/01/16/white-privilege-explained/?utm_term=.299b72797afe.
Eswine, Zack. *Recovering Eden: The Gospel According to Ecclesiastes*. Phillipsburg, NJ: P&R, 2014.
Gire, Ken. *Windows of the Soul: Experiencing God in New Ways*. Grand Rapids: Zondervan, 1996.
Imbach, Jeff. *The River Within*. Colorado Springs, CO: NavPress, 1998.

Bibliography

Kaysen, Susanna. "One Cheer for Melancholy." In *Unholy Ghost: Writers on Depression*, edited by Nell Casey, 38–43 San Francisco: Harper Perennial, 2001.

Kempis, Thomas à. *The Imitation of Christ*. Peabody, MA: Hendrickson, 2004.

Lloyd-Jones, Martyn. *Let Not Your Hearts be Troubled*. Wheaton, IL: Crossway, 2009.

Miller, C. John. *A Faith Worth Sharing: A Lifetime of Conversations about Christ*. Phillipsburg, NJ: P&R, 1999.

Miller, Paul. *Love Walked among Us*. Colorado Springs, CO: NavPress, 2001.

Muggeridge, Malcolm. "The Great Liberal Death Wish." Orthodoxy Today (2002). http://www.orthodoxytoday.org/articles/MuggeridgeLiberal.php.

Newton, John. *Letters of John Newton*. Edinburgh: Banner of Truth Trust, 1960.

"Noise Sources and Their Effects." https://www.chem.purdue.edu/chemsafety/Training/PPETrain/dblevels.htm.

Packer, J. I. *Concise Theology: A Guide to Historic Christian Beliefs*. Orlando, FL: Tyndale, 1993.

———. *Knowing God*. Downers Grove, IL: InterVarsity, 1993.

Palmer, Parker. *To Know as We are Known*. San Francisco: HarperSanFrancisco, 1993.

Peterson, Eugene. *A Long Obedience in the Same Direction*. Downers Grove, IL: InterVarsity, 2000.

———. *The Message (Remix): The Bible in Contemporary Language*. Colorado Springs, CO: NavPress, 2014.

Pulliam Bailey, Sarah. "White Evangelicals Voted Overwhelmingly for Donald Trump, Exit Polls Show." *Washington Post*, November 9, 2016. https://www.washingtonpost.com/news/acts-of-faith/wp/2016/11/09/exit-polls-show-white-evangelicals-voted-overwhelmingly-for-donald-trump/?utm_term=.6b414e14ecff.

Rutledge, Fleming. *Help My Unbelief*. Grand Rapids: Eerdmans, 2000.

Schaeffer, Francis. *True Spirituality*. Wheaton, IL: Tyndale House, 2001.

Stott, John. *Evangelical Truth*. Downers Grove, IL: InterVarsity, 1999.

Welch, Edward T. *Running Scared: Fear, Worry, and the God of Rest*. Greensboro, NC: New Growth, 2007.

Wesley, Charles. "And Can it Be That I Should Gain." In *Trinity Hymnal*, Hymn 455. Suwanee, GA: Great Commission, 1990.

Wright, Richard. *Why Buddhism is True*. New York: Simon and Schuster, 2017.

Yancey, Philip. *What's so Amazing about Grace?* Grand Rapids: Zondervan, 1997.

Zahl, Paul. *Grace in Practice*. Grand Rapids: Eerdmans, 2007.

www.ingramcontent.com/pod-product-compliance
Lightning Source LLC
Chambersburg PA
CBHW050827160426
43192CB00010B/1927